FAMILY CHANGE
AND THE LIFE COURSE
IN JAPAN

by
SUSAN ORPETT LONG

East Asia Program
Cornell University
Ithaca, New York 14853

The *Cornell East Asia Series* (formerly *Cornell
University East Asia Papers*) publishes manuscripts
on a wide variety of scholarly topics pertaining to
East Asia. Manuscripts are published on the basis
of camera-ready copy provided by the volume author
or editor.

Inquiries should be addressed to Editorial Board,
East Asia Series, East Asia Program, Cornell
University, 140 Uris Hall, Ithaca, New York 14853-
7601.

This essay was prepared for a conference sponsored by the Joint Committee on Japanese Studies of the American Council of Learned Societies and the Social Science Research Council. Support was provided by the Japan-United States Friendship Commission.

CONTENTS

List of Tables   vi
List of Figures   vii
Foreword by Glen H. Elder, Jr.   ix
Acknowledgements   xv

THE LIFE COURSE APPROACH   1

The Life Course   3

JAPANESE CONCEPTIONS OF FAMILY   7

Ie and Dōzoku: An Indiginous Approach to Family Studies
    in Japan   10
Legacy of the Indigenous Approach   14

FAMILY STUDIES AND A FAMILY CHANGE FROM A HISTORICAL PERSPECTIVE   15

Periods of Japanese History   15
Resources   18
The Work of Post-War Historians on the Family   22

SOCIOLOGICAL PERSPECTIVES ON FAMILY CHANGE   33

An Overview of Family Sociology in Japan   33
Change in Family Form   39
Mate Selection and Marriage   41
Wives and Husbands   46
Parents and Children   52
Succession   58
The Elderly and Their Family Relations   62
Kinship Relations   75
Opinions About the Family   79

FAMILY CYCLE AND LIFE COURSE IN JAPAN   81

The Family Cycle Framework   81
Life Course Research on Japan   83

THE FUTURE: THE JAPANESE FAMILY AND THE LIFE COURSE APPROACH   87

Social Change and the Japanese Family   87
Japanese Family Studies and the Life Course Approach   89

Bibliography   93
Index of Japanese Terms   117

TABLES

1. Measures of Fertility, Mortality and Population Increase
   for Selected Pre-Modern Japanese Villages   27

2. References to Tokugawa Demographic Studies by Life Cycle
   Stage   28

3. Changes in Household Composition   40

4. Engagement Period Experience of Married Women   43

5. Type of Marriage by Age   45

6. Change in Average Number of Children Per Family   54

7. Support for "Compensatory" Inheritance Among Persons
   60 Years and Older   61

8. Attitudes Toward Adoption   61

9. Changes in Japanese Average Life Expectancy   63

10. Changes in Population Structure   64

11. Reason for Co-residence   67

12. A Comparison of Survey Results on Communality in Three-
    Generation Families   70

13. Reasons for Separate Residence   71

14. Trends in Support of Elderly Living Expenses   72

15. Percentages of Relatives (of All Relatives) with Whom
    Respondents Enter into Social Association of Various
    Types   75

16. Percentages of Relatives (of All Relatives) with Whom
    Respondents Co-operate for Various Items of Help   75

17. Responses to Whether People Would Take In Grandmother   76

18. Systematization of Kinship Relations - A Comparison of
    the Ie and the Modern Family   78

FIGURES

1. Change in Mean Household Size   39

2. Type of Marriage by Age   44

3. Change in Average Age at First Marriage and Age
     Differences of Spouses   47

4. Female Employees by Marital Status   51

5. Japanese Women's Model Life Cycle   53

6. Is It Best for Parents to Live with Their
     Adult Children?   57

7. Trends in Households with Persons Aged 65 and Over   65

vii

FOREWORD

Few topics have aroused more interest in contemporary social science than the course of family change. Some of this interest is prompted in Japan by the concerns of a rapidly changing society, such as the decline of three generation households and the growing problem of the aged. However, family change has long claimed prominence among Japanese studies, an observation well supported by Susan Long's thoughtful survey, Family Change and the Life Course in Japan. Over the years, outstanding studies of the Japanese family have centered on social change. They include Hayami's historical demography of a pre-industrial village, Aruga's investigation of family and kinship in the village of Ishigami, and Smith's account of social change in the postwar village of Kurusu. Though restricted to a point in time, Koyama's important comparative study of a mountain village, a suburban community, and a metropolitan apartment area is at least suggestive on the nature of family change.

Traditionally, studies have investigated change along a single temporal dimension, either historical or family. From the perspective of long-term development, family change is portrayed in terms of functional differentiation and specialization. The specialized nuclear family is one result of this process. Studies have described family patterns at points along the historical time-line and across different settings in the same era. By contrast, a family-time approach too often explores trajectories from marriage to the death or separation of a spouse. Families are compared across ordered stages, usually without regard for the broader social changes that influence their course.

Historical and developmental perspectives refer to processes that are basic to an understanding of family change, and both are represented in Long's survey of Japanese family studies. These strands also come together in an approach to the life course, a framework which emerged during the 1960's in response to an increasing awareness of the relation between social history and life history. Just as change in people and families reflects a changing society, social change occurs in part through change in people. This interaction is represented by the theoretical traditions of age and kinship studies.

Age locates families in historical context by using the birth years of the head and places them socially according to age-graded events, such as

ix

marriage and retirement. The notion of social or family time refers to the ordering of events and roles by age-related expectations, sanctions, and options. Problematic features of the life course arise from the interlocking careers of family members and their patterns of reciprocity and synchrony on needs and resources. Multiple careers in the life course imply multiple worlds whose demands compete for scarce family resources - time, energy, space, affection, money.

This approach to the family is some distance from the primitive models in use before the age of life-course studies. One such model represents a career, a trajectory or pathway that a person, couple, or family follows. Some years ago (1977) I wrote that "traditionally, the life course of an individual has been viewed in terms of a single life path, such as the course of a person's worklife or marriage." Not too long ago, studies of family events and economic conditions largely proceeded along separate paths without acknowledging their interdependence. Today we see far less of a tendency to view family careers in splendid isolation.

A second approach uses life histories, the sequential record of experience that is marked off by events. Research has used this record to understand both husband and wife as persons with a history at the point of marriage. The relative standing of husband and wife reflects such histories, including the difference in status of each spouse's family. Within the context of family studies, the life history perspective has focused attention on the problematic interdependence of lives, past and future, though it offers no conceptual guidance in studying family organization.

A third model of rudimentary design is best known as the family cycle, a kinship perspective which broadens the life course approach beyond a single life span. The family cycle describes a process by which one generation is succeeded by another; parents give birth, grow old, and are replaced by their offspring. The pathway is marked by the ages of children and by a sequence of stages from birth through the dependency years, departure from home, and the birth of another generation. To a considerable extent, personal events among offspring structure the life course of parents, such as childbirth and the parent's transition to grandparent status. By extending the generational framework, we end up with a lineage of surviving kin - parents, grandparents, and even great grandparents. The boundaries of the lineal spread are marked by the youngest dyad of the parent and child and by the oldest dyad of late middle-aged parents and their surviving parents. The youngest member of a four-generation family can anticipate moving across four generational stations in his or her lifetime.

Moving beyond the limitations of career and life history, the life course perspective offers a view of interdependent lives in family dynamics. Family processes evolve over a relatively long span of time, as represented by the concept of trajectory, career, or pathway, and also over a short span, as in transitions from one state to another. Trajectories of work, marriage, and parenthood are interrelated paths that structure the life course of individuals, couples, and family units. By viewing families from the vantage point of interlocking careers, we capture some dynamic features of the family and household economy. Family coordination of member careers depends in part on the appropriate timing of events and demands.

The conceptual meanings of age and the life course include the timing of events, their order or sequence, and the duration of particular states. Timing refers to events and roles within the life course, and to the historical setting of this process, as defined by birth year. An orientation to the social facts of age directs attention to the context of family life and to historical influences in family change. These meanings of age identify a major limitation of family cycle studies. Couples move across the stages without information on their timing and duration. Lacking such distinctions, it is not possible to investigate the way in which families manage activities and lives across time and space. This deficiency also leads to the neglect of historical context and its study in relation to family change.

This brief excursion across distinctions and approaches offers a context in which to place Susan Long's valuable survey of studies of family change in Japan. By organizing her review according to type of data, historical versus contemporary or sociological, she provides an instructive guide across the two principal time-lines, the historical dimension and the family or developmental dimension. Japanese research on past time has largely involved demographic specialists from various disciplines, the use of historical documents such as population registers, and a temporal emphasis on Japanese families prior to industrialization. A large share of this work also views the family across stages of the family cycle, such as marriage without children to older age. Although this does not ensure a processual account of the family, a developmental view of Japanese families in past time is possible by using annual village records, as Hayami's work shows.

Unfortunately, the popularity of the cross-sectional survey in data collection and the appeal of high-level theory (e.g., structure-function, etc.) did not favor a developmental or historical approach to the family in the postwar era. Sociological studies attempted to represent family change across the life span by describing families in different stages. Implied in this practice is the assumption that families in stage B will resemble families who are now in stage A. That is, the sequence should tell us something about the actual course families will follow from marriage to old age. However, change from one family stage to another may reflect both the normative aging of families/individuals and historical change. Cross-sectional surveys do not enable us to determine which explanation is correct.

By the end of the 1970's, the prominence of social change issues led a number of Japanese sociologists to explore ways of studying change in the family and life course. The United States soon became one leg of a comparative framework, with its leadership on indicators of change - women's employment, divorce, and the one-parent household. Using funds from the Japan Society for the Promotion of Science and from the Social Science Research Council of United States, a planning session in Tokyo (December, 1980) brought both Japanese and American social scientists together on matters of family study. Kiyomi Morioka led the team of Japanese sociologists. Historian Tamara Hareven, anthropologist David Plath, and sociologist Reuben Hill represent the American social scientists. Out of this meeting came a decision to launch a bi-national comparative study of the family from a life course perspective. To support this collaborative effort, the planning group made arrangements for another bi-national meeting in America and a final conference in Hawaii. Across this time period, the group also set up exchange visits to both countries.

Initial work on the project soon made clear the need for a thorough overview of family studies in Japan, both sociological and historical. An English-language overview was not available at the time, and the American participants did not have the essential facility in Japanese or mastery over the field of Japanese studies. Susan Long came to our assistance with a draft of the present volume. The bi-national project found the volume so helpful that we sought ways of making it more widely available, from the comparative researcher to graduate and undergraduate students who desire an overview of family studies in Japan. This splendid edition exceeds our expectations and hopefully establishes an important first step toward more comparative research among students of the family in the two societies.

Glen H. Elder, Jr.
Howard W. Odum
Distinguished Professor of
    Sociology

Chapel Hill, North Carolina
November, 1986

ACKNOWLEDGEMENTS

This review was undertaken as part of a larger effort to encourage cross-national and cross-cultural comparisons of family change. In 1982, I was approached by a staff member of the Social Science Research Council to assist the American team in their Project on Japan-U.S. Comparisons of the Family and the Life Course. The Japanese scholars involved in the project were already thoroughly familiar with the analytic frameworks utilized by their American counterparts. The Americans, however, knew little of the literature from which their Japanese colleagues worked. Faced with the formidable barriers of the Japanese language and unfamiliar cultural assumptions, they turned for assistance to two eminent scholars of Japan, Robert J. Smith and David W. Plath, who served as guides and discussants for the project. My task was to provide a background paper which would place the work of the Japanese participants in the project in the broad context of family studies in Japan, and serve as an introduction to research on family change in Japan for the American participants, acquainting them with key concepts, methodologies, and resources.

A number of the American sociologists and social historians subsequently suggested that I revise the survey, which they felt would be useful for their own research and for student reference in graduate courses on the family. The revision, directed toward a broader audience of American researchers and students interested in the Japanese family, assumes that the reader has little or no background in Japanese studies. My hope is that many readers will include Japanese case materials in cross-national family research, thus achieving one of the goals of the original SSRC project.

I have been assisted in this project in numerous ways. Discussions with Ronald Aqua, Tamara Hareven, the late Reuben Hill, John Modell, and David Plath increased my understanding of life course work in the U.S. and aided me in defining the scope and content of the review. Laurel Cornell, Reuben Hill, David Plath, and Ronald Toby helped in identifying and locating materials, as did librarians at the University of Illinois, Western Illinois University, the University of Minnesota, the University of Michigan, and John Carroll University. Members of the Japanese team have been helpful in sending me copies of their publications, especially Masaoka Kanji, Ishihara Kunio, and

Meguro Yoriko. Ikeda Keiko, Fujimoto Nobuko, and Masuda Kōkichi assisted me with the readings of some of the Japanese names.

My understanding of the historical material was enhanced through conversations with Susan B. Hanley, Hayami Akira, and Robert J. Smith. David Plath, Robert Smith, Ronald Toby, John Campbell, Masuda Kōkichi, Fujimoto Nobuko, Kim King, and several anonymous reviewers read all or portions of the earlier draft and contributed many suggestions and insights that have been incorporated into this version. Robert Smith, Glen Elder, and Theodore Bestor assisted with publication planning. The costs of the additional research to update the original report and prepare the manuscript for publication have been met by a travel grant from the Northeast Asia Regional Council of the Association for Asian Studies. Verna Sandall, Robert Baylor, Adrianne Jackson, Carolyn Clifford, and Elizabeth Zitnik assisted with the difficult job of typing and preparing the manuscript for publication. I am grateful to all of these individuals for their assistance.

THE LIFE COURSE APPROACH

In recent years, American scholarship on the family has drawn from diverse disciplinary and theoretical frameworks, as researchers have developed a new approach known as the life course perspective. Sociologists, social historians, and anthropologists utilizing this approach attempt to link the development of the individual with that of the family, and to see both of these processes embedded in historical and cultural context. They investigate changes at both the macro and the micro levels, asking how they affect individual roles and careers through the mediation of the family and other social institutions.

In the past decade or two, researchers have produced numerous books and articles on the life course perspective. These deal with theoretical issues and with empirical data from various American and Western European populations. These studies have stimulated an interest in the life course approach and related methodologies on the part of some Japanese historians and sociologists who have an interest in family change. The first large scale study in Japan explicitly using the life course perspective was initiated in 1981 in Shizuoka by a group of Japanese sociologists. The first Japanese language text on the life course in Japanese is scheduled for publication in the mid-1980's (Morioka and Aoi, in press).

This review is designed to serve several purposes. It introduces the study of family change in Japan by selectively reviewing Japanese research related to life course concerns. Although some Japanese scholars have published in English, much of their material is available only in Japanese. Americans who study Japan from a comparative perspective often focus on issues of continuity and cross-cultural differences; Japanese researchers examining their own society are more interested in the process and meaning of change. Sociologists have documented the tremendous changes in the Japanese family that have accompanied urbanization and economic growth since World War II, a process they call the "nuclearization" of the family. Historians point out, however, that changes in form and function of the family characterize earlier times as well. Scholars of both disciplines look to wider social change, particularly economic development, for causal explanations of family change.

A second goal of the survey is to present a critical assessment of the "state of the art" of Japanese studies of family change, as these studies bear on new interests in the life course. I thus provide the context of the research I review, its historical development, methods, and assumptions. I hope to make it easier for American researchers to include Japan in their discussions of the life course, and to foster individual and collaborative cross-national research.

To include all research on family change in Japan would not only be a monumental undertaking, it would detract from the focus on life course concerns. I attempt to present a range of approaches and methodologies, but the practicalities of locating documents may have lent a bias to what material I have been able to include. I carried out research at several excellent East Asian collections in the U.S. as well as in the personal libraries of several scholars. However, I have been limited to working in the U.S. and to analyzing materials which individual Japanese scholars themselves have sent to me. In those cases where I have not had access to the original reports or books, but have relied on reviews of them by other Japanese scholars, I so indicate in the text or references. Where a publication in English approximates the material available in a Japanese article, I have cross-referenced both in the bibliography. Japanese names are written in the Japanese manner, surname first. For greater ease in locating material, reference to work by an institute or organization is given in Japanese if it is a Japanese language publication and in English if the report is in English.

Since I have assumed that my readers have little background in Japanese studies, I first review some of the key concepts and assumptions concerning the Japanese family. In any attempt at cross-cultural understanding, defining terms that do not translate easily is an important step. Therefore, I discuss a number of Japanese words, kazoku, shinrui, ie, and dōzoku, which are critical for an understanding of the Japanese literature. It is also important to know how to deal with these terms in assessing the "fit" of Western life course concepts to the Japanese case.

The major part of volume is divided into two sections, historical and sociological. This does not imply the existence of a sharp division between historical and modern studies; in fact, many of the sociologists are explicitly concerned with historical change. Rather, the basis for the division is methodological. The historians rely primarily on pre-modern documents and early census data. The sociologists conduct survey research, analyzing change by observing differences in aggregate responses through time. Their work is primarily cross-sectional, and there are few follow-up studies or multigenerational projects.

Chapter 3 is a review of the historical approach. I deal with the Tokugawa (1600-1867) and Meiji (1868-1912) periods because the work relates directly to the life course perspective and because these periods tie in best with the sociological approach, representing the "traditional", as opposed to the "modern" of the postwar period. I first describe these two periods in general terms and justify the use of this periodization in family studies. I next discuss the methods used and resources available for the study of premodern family change in these periods. I summarize this work and relate various studies to each other and to a broader view of the life course.

The sociological approach is reviewed in Chapter 4. After an overview of Japanese family sociology and an introduction to variables used and resources available, I review the literature in seven subject areas: change in family form, mate selection and marriage, husband-wife relations, parent-child relations, succession, the elderly and their families, and relatives. These divisions are based on the way Japanese family sociologists have subdivided the field. I then briefly introduce the two theoretical perspectives of greatest interest, the older family cycle approach and the new life course approach. In the final section, I return to some of the questions raised by the life course approach. Although publications directly utilizing this new perspective are only beginning to appear, the scholarly work I have reviewed provides a strong base for further development of life course work in Japan. The Japanese data may also help us refine the approach so that it will be increasingly useful for comparing human lives across various times and places.

The Life Course

The life course perspective does not imply a single focus or a specific methodology. As Hagestad and Neugarten (1985:39) have put it, "The search for a conceptual framework that is appropriate to the study of age systems and the life course in modern societies, one that relates them to other phenomena such as historical change and subgroup differences, is still underway." Life course work generally concentrates on one of three levels of analysis: the individual, the family or other groups of individuals, or the perceptions and symbols found in a particular cultural context.

At the level of the individual, the accent is on the person as an active creator of his or her life course, within the bounds of circumstance. "The life course refers to pathways which individuals follow through age-differentiated roles and events... life course is multidimensional since movement through successive life stages entails the concurrent assumption of multiple roles" (Elder 1977:282). Each role may have successive stages, a career. Some roles become inappropriate, while others are added. Plath (1982) emphasizes that while some sequences of roles are institutionally based, humans also experience a succession of individual achievements not technically considered a career but which, personally experienced and created, establish a culturally recognized pathway to maturity.

When the individual is viewed as having these multiple careers over time, research addresses the timing and sequencing of a person's careers over the life span. A person makes conscious choices, to postpone marriage in order to establish an occupational career, for example, but social norms and the careers of intimate others directly affect such decisions. The key concept in much of this research is that of transition, turning points or role changes of personal and social significance for the life course. Research addresses questions of patterning and variability in the timing, spacing, and sequencing of transitions in different gender, ethnic, socioeconomic, and historical populations.

A second level of analysis stresses the interrelationship of an individual's life course with that of people closest to him or her. These "consociates" (Plath 1980) influence a person's opportunities through their own role performances and career decisions; they are also the most direct source of age-related norms which indicate to a person his own timeliness. Transitions are not only markers in individual careers, but are "socially created, socially recognized, and shared" (Hagestad and Neugarten 1985:35). If our consociates are those who grow old with us, as Plath has described them, then we can locate individuals in a historical context as well.

A family, in this sense, can be thought of as a co-biography of its members. Research centers on the synchronizing of multiple careers of several individuals in response to perceived problems of resource management (Elder 1977). Normative timetables for transitions of a family or its members have changed historically. A normatively late transition, such as late parenting, has repercussions for the timing of not only the individual's other careers,

but for the careers of consociates as well, since if your child does not become a parent, you cannot become a grandparent. Other transitions, such as
widowhood, are less a consequence of purposeful decisions, but nonetheless
depend upon the transition of another.

The third level of analysis deals with the cultural phenomenology of the
life course. It relates the subjective meanings of transitions (autobiography) to the social context by focusing on the ideas and symbols by which people interpret events. As Plath (1981) reflects, we need to discover how "people grow out of socialization as well as into it." Researchers also have
asked about the perceived periods of life and their characteristics, markers,
and evaluations. This area, the relation of individual interpretations of the
life course to cultural definitions seems to have received the least attention
in empirical life course work.

Finally, there remains the question of the antecedents of the life course
approach. Elder (1977) traces its sociological roots to the study of individual histories and careers, especially by sociologists of the early "Chicago
school" in the 1920's and 1930's, who stressed historical context and the process of social change. The single most influential work is The Polish Peasant
in Europe and America by William I. Thomas and F. Znaniecki, published by the
University of Chicago Press in 1918-20 (Elder 1977:281-1). Hareven (1982b)
points to the development of interest in biography and oral history. Hagestad
and Neugarten (1985) trace the development of the sociology of age differentiation to ethnographic studies of age grading and the attribution of social
meaning to the passage of life time. The development of life span psychology
has also contributed to life course concepts.

Life course research utilizes a number of methods, as the array of con-
tributing disciplines suggests. Historians make use of historical demographic
techniques, including the analysis of population registers, and life history
analysis. Sociologists have collected life histories and longitudinal data,
and developed new multigenerational methodologies. They have also relied
heavily on cohort analysis of cross-sectional data to produce statistical
portraits of the life course. To this great variety of material, researchers
bring an approach which seeks to explain individual lives in historical and
sociocultural context.

JAPANESE CONCEPTIONS OF THE FAMILY

A major problem hindering cross-cultural research involves the translation of key concepts. In this chapter, I take up a number of Japanese conceptions of family. In the United States, family generally refers to a nuclear family composed of parent(s) and unmarried child(ren). The term is also used to refer to some less well-defined circle of relations extending beyond that unit. I deal in this section first with those Japanese concepts most closely related to the first American meaning, and secondly with concepts which include a broader circle of relatives. Finally, I note implications of Japanese-United States differences for life course studies. The key difference is the Japanese emphasis on lineality. Most adult Americans include brothers and sisters as "family" in the broader sense. In Japan, siblings belong to the same family as children. Although they remain relatives (see discussion of kindred, page 10), adult siblings may be considered members of separate families.

Kazoku. This term is probably the closest to the English "family", referring to people related by blood, marriage, or adoption who share household residence. According to Kōjien, a major Japanese language dictionary, the term may refer to members of an ie (see below), but the first definition is, "a relation of people tied by blood and living together, a unit of social organization based on marriage," suggesting that it is the nuclear family which is most often implied by the word kazoku. Sociologically, the emphasis on the conjugal bond in this definition stands in contrast to the main emphasis on lineality that characterizes the conception of ie.

Ie. Common usage of this term for both "house" and its residents suggests the most common translation of ie into English: household. However, this translation provides none of the cultural nuances (for example, the sense of "old-fashioned" has been expressed by many young Japanese), nor does it explain its place in Japanese academic work.

As an academic concept, ie is a multigenerational property-owning corporate group which continues through time. Its structure is that of the stem family, a three generation family in which there only one married couple from each generation together with their unmarried children. However, membership in the Japanese stem family is not limited to direct descendents, but includes those brought in through marriage, adoption or fictive kin relations (such as servants). Japanese sociologists refer to it as chokkei kazoku, or

- 7 -

"lineal family", thus emphasizing continuity and time-depth. As Aruga (1954:362) explains:

Ancestors and offspring are linked together by an idea of family geneology,... which does not mean relationships based on mere blood inheritance and succession, but rather a bond of relationship inherent in the maintenance and continuance of the family as an institution.

Roles within this institution overlap with, but are not limited to, kinship relations. Authority is concentrated in the role (not the person) of household head, a position usually occupied by the eldest living male. We might consider the headship equivalent to that of household manager, who supervises the daily activities of the ie and who represents the ie (as the basic social unit of society) in the larger community. Although he has ultimate authority over other ie members, his decisions should be made in the best interest of the ie as a whole.

Among the sacred duties of the head... was that of preserving the descent line unbroken. He was responsible for passing on, enlarged if possible, the goods and property he had inherited, and it was his duty to see to the proper veneration of the ancestors. (Smith 1978b:45-46)

The wife of the household head, as well as the designated successor and his wife, have specific responsibilities and realms of authority.

Property-ownership lies at the core of the ie institution. Usually ie property included living quarters, household goods, and the "means of production necessary for a family occupation" (Aoi and Yuzawa 1981:5). In the case of rural ie, means of production meant rights to land use, tools, and equipment. The family head supervised, as his most important duty, the training of a successor in the skills necessary to carry on the ie occupation. He also arranged for the livelihoods of non-successors, the marriage of all children and an occupational start for sons. Succession, including both inheritance of property and taking over of the position of head, occurred at the death or the retirement of the head. In the not uncommon situation in which there was no suitable biological heir, a yōshi was adopted as heir to the ie property and occupation. (Since a yōshi was often brought in as husband to a daughter of an ie, the term is often translated as "adopted son-in-law." However, yōshi did not always marry into the family; I prefer to translate yōshi as "adopted successor," emphasizing the motivation for the adoption.) The material bonds of ie were reinforced ideologically by ancestor worship, family crests, and other symbols of the ie.

As described above, the ie is an abstraction, grounded in observed behavior, but elevated to the level of a sociological model. (See discussions in Laslett 1973 and 1978, Hareven 1982a, and Verdon 1983 concerning the stem family model in the West.) It is this model which served as the basis for family law in the pre-World War II period. In fact, much of the development of and empirical research on this model took place during this period. Many contemporary scholars thus view it as a highly conservative and often distasteful approach to "family". To some Japanese researchers, the ie reflects "feudal" or "imperialistic" stages of Japanese society, and they are anxious to show its breakdown in the modern era.

I next turn to two concepts related to the broader meaning of family as a group of relatives not sharing a common household.

Dōzoku. This is a corporate group composed not of individuals, but of hierarchically related ie units. Like ie, it is a model abstracted from observed behavior; but unlike ie, dōzoku is not itself a folk term. It was created by social scientists to explain similar aspects of social organization that are known by various names in different parts of the country.

Because relationships among the ie are modeled on geneological relationships, the dōzoku has often been considered a patrilineal descent group. The main ie, at the apex of the pyramid, is called honke. Other ie known as branch families or bunke, come to have a dependent relationship with the main ie in one of several ways. Often the bunke originate with the household head of the main ie setting up a branch family for non-successor children (usually sons) by providing them with land or other means of livelihood. The same may be done for servants. These branch families, while nuclear in form for the first generation, become stem families by the second and may even create their own bunke in later generations, though they, too, would recognize their subordinate position vis-a-vis the original main household. The twin criteria of economic dependency (at least originally) and the recognition of reciprocal asymmetrical obligations determine the dōzoku relationship. A third way of becoming a bunke is for a family without dōzoku ties of its own to request such a relationship with the main ie and to formally acknowledge its dependency on and obligations to it. However, dōzoku, unlike lineages or clans, are not defined by rules of exogamy.

The honke, aside from providing the branch with the means of livelihood such as land rights for farmers or branch shops for merchants, continues to have responsibility for the welfare of its members. The main household head

provides economic assistance for <u>bunke</u> and serves as go-between for marriage
of their children. In exchange, the <u>bunke</u> provide labor services and are
obligated to participate in ancestor worship or other rites of the main <u>ie</u>.
Such obligations are not restricted to the first generation <u>bunke</u>, but continue as part of <u>ie</u> "property" through time.

<u>Kindred</u>. In contrast to the corporate, permanent nature of dōzoku rela-
tionships, Japanese sociologists recognize another type of relationship known
by a variety of terms, most commonly <u>shinrui</u>, <u>shinzoku</u> or <u>shinseki</u>. This is
an egocentric bilateral circle of relatives which may overlap with dōzoku
ties, but extends beyond these by including mother's relatives, father's sister's relatives, and in-laws (including wife's and daughter-in-law's relatives). Degrees of geneological closeness are often distinguished, but locality is the primary determinant of the relationship. Although not obligatory
in the sense of dōzoku obligations, kindred provide mutual support through
economic assistance, participation in life crisis ceremonies (especially funerals), and ritual visiting (Befu 1963).

In anthropological kinship studies, bilateral kinship reckoning and patrilineal descent groups are usually viewed as mutually exclusive in a given
society. Although Japanese scholars disagree as to its meaning (see below),
there is no doubt that both principles have operated simultaneously in
Japanese society, though with varying, and inversely related, strength in
different parts of the country.

Ie and Dōzoku: An Indigenous Approach to Family Studies in Japan

In spite of the political overtones of <u>ie</u> and dōzoku, Japanese scholars
have recognized the utility of these concepts for comparisons with other societies and for explaining social change.

Academic concern with <u>ie</u> seems to date to the early work of Yanagita
Kunio in the 1920's to 1940's. Yanagita's work lies on the boundary of our
categories of folklore and ethnography. He and his students conducted numerous field surveys in various parts of Japan to collect information on local
customs and dialects. His concern was largely atheoretical and his analytical
methods inductive. His sense of mission seems to have been to capture what
was unique about Japanese life in the face of rapid social change. He was
political in that his goal was to document Japan's cultural roots as distinct

from their Chinese and Western influences and from the samurai ethos propagated by the state since 1868 which obscured the "true" roots of Japanese custom. He viewed the ie as a stage in the historical progression from the very large family to the small family. Yet, he did not regard the ie of the 20th century as a mere survival from former times; he believed it to have continuing functions in the family life of the modern Japanese. He approached the ie from two separate interests: looking at the process of family change from the perspective of the organization of the agricultural labor force; and as the basis of the folk belief in ancestor worship, which he saw as the desire to perpetuate the ie (Morita 1979).

Yanagita's influence was felt most strongly in sociology through Aruga Kizaemon, considered the father of family studies in Japan. (There is controversy in Japan as to whether this name should be romanized as Aruga or Ariga. I have used the former, but references may be found in the literature under either spelling.) Following Yanagita, Aruga argued that the ie or large family was the major Japanese family form, and that the patriarchal power supporting it has been greatly weakened by the development of a capitalist economy and by post-war revisions in the civil code. Another sociologist, Oikawa Hiroshi, first defined the basic unit of dōzoku as the ie and recognized the dominant-subordinate relationship as the principle of dōzoku organization (Koyano 1976:37). But it was Aruga who solidified the concepts of ie and dōzoku and related them to wider economic, political and historical forces, particularly the relation between the land tenure system and dōzoku. Nakane claims that Aruga's study of Ishigami village over a 30 year period resulted in "the best sociological monograph that has been produced in Japan" (Nakane 1967:176).

Aruga stressed the economic factors involved in creating and maintaining ie and dōzoku. Another sociologist, Kitano Seiichi, focused on these institutions as kinship organizations. He tried to explain the coexistence of dōzoku and kindred by a theory of dual kinship structure. A historical system creates dōzoku, while a synchronic family core results in a bilateral kin group (Koyano 1976:38).

Japanese rural sociologists raised the issue of how both dōzoku and kindred organizations help to integrate the larger community (a rural village). Influenced by Aruga, Fukutake Tadashi noted first of all that the ideal type dōzoku is rarely found, and when it is, it is in the least economically developed areas. On the other hand, as dōzoku declined in importance in community

organization, kindred relations increased in importance. He thus developed a
typology of 1) villages hierarchically structured by dōzoku, and 2) villages
without dōzoku in which land holdings were more equally distributed and in
which kindred ties were more important as a mechanism for community integra-
tion. This dichotomy corresponded roughly to a geographical division of
Japan, with strong dōzoku found primarily in the northeast and weak or no
dōzoku in the southwest. (For a translation by Ronald Dore of one of
Fukutake's major works, see Fukutake 1967.)

Ironically, as Japanese sociologists turned to American models and methods after World War II, the influence of this indigenous approach to family
can be seen most strongly in the work of American ethnographers (Befu 1962,
1963; Brown 1966, 1979; Cornell 1964; Johnson 1964; Matsumoto 1962; Norbeck
1954, 1978; R. Smith 1956, 1974, 1978b). Like the folklorist-ethnographers,
they desired to explain the uniqueness of Japanese family and village organization, emphasizing contrasts rather than similarities with the West. In utilizing concepts of ie and dōzoku, they have contributed to them, although their
modifications have apparently had little effect in Japanese scholarship
(Nakane 1974:70). I find Brown's discussion (1966) particularly noteworthy.
He distinguishes patrilineal descent as ideology from the actual functioning
of ie and dōzoku in specific contexts which sometimes call for family succession based on branching through females. By recognizing cognatic descent,
such occurrences present no challenge to the dominant ideology. Recently,
Bachnik (1983) argued that position, rather than kinship, is the key to understanding the ie. Position is defined according to five ranked components:
permanency of ie membership, in-group membership, older generation, male, and
birth order. The two permanent members from each generation form the core of
the ie and assure its continuity through time. Recruitment and succession to
these two positions takes place by one of five logically possible strategies.
The socially preferred strategy is succession by the first son and his out-
group wife. But (as other scholars note as well) the continuity and success
of the ie takes precedence, and any of the strategies are acceptable in pur-
suit of these goals.

I would like to turn briefly to studies by two Americans which deal directly with social change to ask what changes they have seen in the Japanese
family. Both Norbeck (1978) and Robert Smith (1978) did rural village ethnog-
raphies in the early 1950's and returned to re-study the same villages approximately 25 years later. Although the two villages differed in their 1950 economic base (farming versus fishing), both authors found extensive changes had

occurred by the mid-1970's. The changes in the family they noted are remarkably similar: a decreased size of family; an increase in the proportion of nuclear families due to the desire of young people to live separately from their parents; a decreased incidence of arranged marriage; an increased proportion of elderly households (without children co-residing). Norbeck further found that the status of women had improved, with most employed for wages. There were no new cases of yōshi (adopted husbands) coming into the family. Because most people are employed in industry, ties with other (not co-residing) kin were much weaker, especially economic ties. The function of kinship in integrating the larger community was vastly decreased.

> Within the residential family, relationships continue to be intimate if otherwise changed. Intimacy is thinned, however, by growing contacts with people outside the family, and changed roles of kin accompanied by changed conceptions of the right and proper behavior among kin have tempered the nature of the whole realm of kinship. Fathers are less commanding, mothers less meekly submissive, children less bound by ideals of filial piety, and mothers-in-law -- the mothers of married sons -- have ceased to hold strong control over their sons' wives. No mother-in-law wishes to gain a reputation in this respect as being a traditional tyrant and thus bring upon herself the demeaning charge of being "left behind the times" and "feudal." In any case, the number of new or recent brides who live with their husbands' parents has become small.
>
> Eldest sons long ago lost their thrones, in some measure acceding them to younger brothers and even sisters. Eldest sons are still often expected to remain at home and, when the time comes, to care for their aged parents. Younger sons may go elsewhere, where economic opportunities are better and where they are unencumbered by the responsibility of caring for aged parents. (Norbeck 1978:300)

Smith noted that spouses are now being selected from a wider geographical range. Both find continuity in the extreme flexibility of succession practices.

I mention briefly one other person who has worked in the ethnographic tradition, Nakane Chie. Although trained in British social anthropology and so viewing herself in a quite separate tradition from family sociology, she nonetheless deals with the indigenous concepts of ie and dōzoku. Nakane rejects much of the earlier work, claiming that the principle of patrilineal descent is a myth in Japanese culture. Rather, she identifies as the basis of family and village organization the localized descent group which reflects external economic conditions and which is limited in membership by residence in the community (Nakane 1967).

Legacy of the Indigenous Approach

Although contemporary Japanese family sociologists trace their academic geneology primarily to Toda (see Chapter 4), they are also conscious heirs of the large household approach. They utilize the ie-dōzoku model as the standard "traditional family" from which they trace changes in the direction of the "modern" nuclear family. Furthermore, the questions many researchers ask are derived from the ie model, such as the extent of adoption, succession patterns, the nature of mother-in-law -- daughter-in-law relations, and the keeping (or not keeping) of ancestral tablets.

The indigenous perspective of the Japanese scholars presents several challenges to the life course approach developing in the United States. It forces us to recognize the complexity of definitions of family. Families are not always nuclear in form, and moreover, recognizing a single principle of descent (for example, patrilineal descent) may be overly simplistic.

In that the ie model to some extent reflected actual behavior, it suggests that the set of transitions to be considered by life course scholars may vary culturally and historically. Birth of first son might be more meaningful in some cases, for example, than birth of first child. We need to add to our repertoire the transitions of adoption, succession, and retirement. Non-kin householders should or should not be included in family, depending on the circumstances, and fictive kin relations need to be examined more closely.

FAMILY STUDIES AND FAMILY CHANGE
FROM A HISTORICAL PERSPECTIVE

In this section, I identify several types of materials which I believe are of interest in gaining a long-term perspective on the family and the life course in Japan. Initially, I describe some of the source material available for historical, demographic, and legal research. I then turn to a discussion of the major work that has been done in this area. First, however, I would like to digress for a moment to discuss periodicity.

Periods of Japanese History

Both Japanese and Western scholars appear to accept divisions of institutional/political history represented by changes of political regime. Although some materials are available from earlier periods, most historical interest in the family has focused on the period after 1600 A.D. I will briefly characterize the major post-1600 eras and then speculate as to the utility of these divisions in the study of family change.

Tokugawa Era, 1600 - 1868. This period is named after the powerful military family which after gaining control of most of Japan, established a government in Edo (now Tokyo; Edo is the more commonly used term for this period in Japanese writing). While the Imperial family remained, powerless, in Kyoto, the Tokugawa Shōguns established a system of government which has been frequently characterized as "centralized feudalism." Territorial feudal lords (daimyō) retained a large degree of autonomy within their domains, but their power was severely restricted by national laws and by the economic requirements of the Edo government. The government severely limited its foreign relations, so that the period is often characterized as "sakoku" or "closed country." To help maintain social control, Christianity was outlawed and all families were required to register as members of a Buddhist temple (see below). A rigidly structured Confucian class system was instituted with accompanying sumptuary and behavioral rules: samurai, farmer, artisan, merchant, with a few other categories of people such as outcasts below these (Hall 1975).

Although pre-war and Marxist historians have depicted the Tokugawa period as one of feudal stagnation, post-war research has demonstrated significant vitality. It was a period of peace, converting the warrior class into bureaucrats and managers. Moreover, economic growth and change was "gradual but

constant" (see Hanley and Yamamura's review article, 1971). The commercial-
ization of the economy and increased agricultural productivity meant higher
standards of living and broader horizons for peasants and the emergence of an
urban middle class. Tokugawa society was highly urbanized by contemporary
international standards. Whereas in 1700, only 2% of the population of Europe
resided in cities of more than 100,000 people, 5 - 7% of the Japanese population lived in cities of that size. Edo alone had a population of one million,
and Kyoto and Osaka each had 400,000 (McClain 1980:267). The literacy rate
was high by contemporary standards as well: by the mid-nineteenth century
about 45% of males were literate (Dore 1965). Scholars turned their attention
first to Confucianism and later to Western science or the new "national studies." Thus, the Tokugawa period has come to be seen by many historians as one
of vast socioeconomic change that led Japan to the point where industrial
take-off could begin.

Meiji Period, 1868 - 1912. The Meiji Restoration was a coup by a group
of samurai that theoretically "restored" the Emperor (whose reign name was
Meiji) to power against the background of Tokugawa socioeconomic changes and
the forced "opening" of Japan to the United States and European powers from
the 1850's. The new government, in the nation's self-defense, rapidly adopted
the military, political, and economic institutions of the West. The class system was abolished, conscription established, and public elementary education
universalized. The government began an intensive industrialization program.
Later in the period, the government's direct involvement in industry was replaced by the growing power of the private sector, especially the zaibatsu
conglomerates. A constitution was written which established a limited
Parliamentary system, conceived of as a gift to the people from the Emperor
who was constitutionally sovereign. Later in the period, political parties
were formed and the franchise expanded. The legal system was modeled on those
of the West, with the exception of the family code which took the core of the
ie system as a model. Internationally, regular relations were established
with other countries, and a policy of military expansionism was begun.

Taishō (1913 - 1926) and early Shōwa (1926 -   ) Periods. The names of
these periods follow the reign names of the Emperors who in reality have had
little political power. Politically and culturally, the period leading up to
World War II showed two conflicting trends, The first was increasing political participation and the emergence of "modern" or "Western" (perhaps "cosmo-
politan" would be a better term) values and lifestyles in the urban areas.

Thus, this period from 1913 - 1932 is sometimes referred to as the era of "Taishō democracy." The other trend, ultimately stronger, was of increased social control at home and military expansionism abroad. For these purposes, the government invoked "traditional" conservative values and authority patterns. The nation came to be conceived of ideologically as one large ie, a "family state" headed by an emperor-father.

Post-War. During the American occupation of Japan, the victors demanded a vast reorganization of the society designed to disarm and democratize the country. Reforms included a new constitution which relegated the Emperor to symbolic status and gave political sovereignty to the people, a vast and effective land reform, attempts to break up the zaibatsu, disbanding the military, and reformulation of the legal and educational systems on American models. Some people have argued that this marked a sharp break with the past, while others suggest that most of these reforms were easily accepted by the public as a logical continuation of pre-war trends as exemplified by the Taishō-Shōwa democracy.

Periodization. Although any divisions of history are in a sense arbitrary, it seems to me useful to continue to utilize at least a 3-period scheme (Tokugawa, pre-war, post-war) in tracing family and life course change after 1600. We may want, however, to define subperiods in family studies differently from those of political history as we review the data.

The major justifications for continued use of the Meiji Restoration and World War II as dividers are legal and economic. For the Tokugawa period, family structure was largely a matter of local (or at most domain-level) governance. Although approval of marriage alliances was required for high-ranking samurai, questions of commoner mate selection, family size, and succession were of little concern as long as taxes were paid and public order maintained. Such decisions thus largely reflected local circumstances. With the Meiji period, however, a national standard was created with the modified ie as model. Sexual inequality and distinction between heir and non-heir descendants (as well as between kin and non-kin household members) were institutionalized. The household head was given absolute authority to decide matters of marriage and divorce of his dependents. Primogeniture, limiting single-heir inheritance to the eldest son, became the rule of succession. In contrast, the post-war reforms removed the entire legal basis of the ie, guaranteeing the rights (if not the practice) of sexual equality, equal inheritance by all children, and freedom of marital and occupational choice. In short, the individual rather than the ie was given legal recognition as the basic social unit. The second argument is an economic one. The Tokugawa economy was highly commercialized, but not yet industrial. Therefore, the organization of labor, while responsive to changing economic conditions, could remain largely household-based (cf. Nakamura 1981). The Meiji period can perhaps be viewed as a time of transition. While the economy was rapidly industrializing, the majority of the population remained employed in agriculture, and the vast majority in the lower section of the dual economic structure (i.e., agriculture, shops, and small business). Given this stability of the population during industrialization, I would expect to find a variety of family patterns, both rural and urban, but a gradual emergence of nuclear-type families if the correlation between industrialization and nuclearization holds. The tendency toward variation would be held in check by the legal standards described above, by universal education and national conscription, and by the mass media (newspapers, magazines, radio). With Japan's economic development in the post-war period came rapid urbanization and a much greater participation in the industrial economy, including that of rural residents and women. Greater standardization of family form and values might emerge from the influence of television and other media, along with the decline in rural-urban and dual economy differences.

Resources

1) Laws and Regulations. While innumerable books are available in Japanese which detail laws or regulations on relevant topics (for example, a recent book by Ishii [1980] is entitled The History of Succession Law in Japan), we are fortunate to have a number of translations and analyses in English which I note here.

Tokugawa. A large collection of legal materials from the Tokugawa period have been translated and edited by John Henry Wigmore under the title Law and Justice in Tokugawa Society. Of special interest are Parts V (1971) and VII (1972). Part V, "Property: Civil Customary Law" includes a section on succession, and distribution of patrimony. Part VII, "Persons: Civil Customary Law," discusses class distinctions, the registration of and rituals surrounding birth, death, marriage, and adoption. It also contains sections on domicile, the definition and obligations of relatives (including legitimacy of

children) and village groups (kumi), and guardianship. Henderson (1975) provides examples of actual village contracts concerning marriage, adoption, and
the hiring of servants. Regulations from the Satsuma domain (southwestern
Japan) concerning the population registration and identification tag system
(see below) are translated in Haraguchi, et al. (1975). These regulations,
and their analysis by Robert Sakai, provide further information on practices
surrounding birth, marriage, death, adoption, and mobility.

Meiji. Nakane (1967:179) notes that Japanese legal scholars have studied
the ie from a comparative legal perspective. The Meiji leaders, in spite of
their modernization program, remained conservative in their ideas about family
and wrote the "traditional" ie system into the Civil Code. Legal scholars,
particularly in the post-war period, have adopted an evolutionary perspective,
viewing the Meiji code as describing feudal pattern which would change into a
more modern family form. The work of Nakagawa, et al. (1955) is probably the
most comprehensive work reflecting the legal approach. Steiner (1950) provides an excellent English summary of Meiji Civil law regarding the family.
Watanabe's (1963) article on the post-war family code discusses the notion of
individuality in the law, in contrast to the Meiji code.

2) Demographic Source Materials. From at least the Tokugawa period,
Japan has had a highly bureaucratic government, a high literacy rate, and a
good supply of paper; numerous records abound from all levels of government,
as well as private records, geneologies, and diaries. (See Yamamura and
Hanley (1972), Crawcour (1961), T. Smith (1959 and 1977), Hiraga (1972) and
Moore (1972) for detailed discussion of various historical records, including
problems of their access and use.)

Several types of records have proven useful to scholars whose work relates well to the family and life course perspective. Sekiyama Naotaro (1958)
began to work with these records, but it is Hayami Akira who applied the family reconstitution methodology to these data. Hayami has influenced other
scholars both in Japan (see, for example Yamada 1984, Narimatsu 1985, Kito
1983) and the United States (work in progress by Ronald Toby, Laurel Cornell,
William Skinner, and James White).

The major sources of data are annual village documents known as the Register of Persons (ninbetsu chō) and the Register of Religious Affiliation
(shūmon aratame chō). The government used the former population surveys for
determining labor services, but in 1671 these were combined with the latter
Registers of Religious Affiliation to become the shūmon ninbetsu aratame chō

(Registers of Religious Affiliation and Population). The registration of religious affiliation was begun originally to enforce the anti-Christian policy of the Tokugawa government, but apparently was discovered to have other uses in control of the population, since they were continued throughout the Tokugawa period. The methodology developed by Hayami (see Hayami 1979) makes use of microfilmed shūmon aratame chō records for a specific village, selected for quality of data and the applicability to the particular questions posed. Researchers then prepare several types of data sheets. A "static" data for each year indicates such factors as age, sex, and marital status composition of all village households. Other data sheets trace households and individuals through the time period covered by the records, which can be used to write household or individual life histories. A separate type of data sheet is used for family reconstitution, as has been done in Europe and North America. Hayami points out that the shūmonchō (at least the ideal ones) can provide the following information for family reconstitution: age at marriage and at end of marriage, term of marriage, reason for end of marriage, age-specific fertility, live births per mother, sex-specific birth order, mother's age at childbirth, birth interval, child and adult mortality. Some registers provide such detail as destination of and reasons (marriage, adoption, work) for village emigration and immigration. Moreover, it is sometimes possible to stratify this information by occupation and size of land holding, which are recorded in some registers.

Smith (1977:18) points out two other population registers which were useful in corroborating or supplementing data from the shūmonchō. The zōgenchō was an annual record of migration into and out of the village which was often kept as a distinct register from the shūmonchō. In addition, some villages kept separate registers of servants, called hōkoninchō. This recorded both those from the village who went to work elsewhere and those coming into the village. Land holding records used for tax purposes may also provide supplementary data if property is not reported in the shūmonchō. It is rare, however, to find all of these records for any one village.

With the Meiji Restoration came changes in record-keeping. In particular, religious freedom was established and thus the rationale for the shūmonchō as temple registers eliminated. Instead, European-style family registers, called koseki, were adopted. Fukushima (1967) analyzes the development of the koseki system, arguing that the koseki supported the ie system, which in turn made possible the development of Japanese capitalism in the

Meiji period. Government officials recorded in the koseki each individual, his/her relation to the family head, and details of his/her birth, marriage, adoption, and death. In the Meiji registers, it is relatively easy to identify and follow up a wide circle of relatives. People who permanently left the household were "erased," but this was done by noting the departure and providing detail on it, not by actually erasing. The koseki remain in use, but are now based on a nuclear family mode. "Erasures" of people leaving the family are complete; a new koseki is begun for each married couple, and no information on them remains in the parent's koseki (Yanase 1972). Yamamura and Hanley (1972) believe modern census records, begun in 1920, to be more reliable than koseki data, but the koseki do provide information from 1871 and can provide other types of information not available in census data such as consanguinity (Yanase 1972:118) and reasons for moving into or out of the household (Fujiki 1972:132).

3) Journals. Several journals available in U.S. libraries contain articles and reviews of interest to family and life course scholars. One, Shakai Keizai Shigaku (Social and Economic History), is an established journal which is generally quantitative in approach. Each issue includes an English table of contents and English abstracts of the major articles. The second journal, entitled Kazoku Shi Kenkyū (Studies of Family History), began semiannual publication only in 1980. Although it does not contain English abstracts, its content is likely to be of interest. Its contents include a "Special Collection," major articles on a common theme (for example, v. 3 The Form and Development of the Ie in Tokugawa Japan; v. 4 The Quickening of the Modern Family in Japan). These are followed by other articles and/or research notes, then book reviews and "literature introduction" of new books. A number of specific references are found in the bibliography. Although some articles deal with family history in other societies, most are concerned with the Japanese family. It claims to be an interdisciplinary journal, including history, sociology, ethnography, folklore studies, legal studies, economics, political science, intellectual history, and analytic psychology. Oikawa (1980) points out that the basic question the journal addresses is the structure and development of the family as an economic unit of society based on private ownership of property.

The Work of Post-War Historians on the Family

Tokugawa. Most historians interested in the family have been economic or agricultural historians. Their basic concerns have been issues such as the land ownership system, the organization of labor, and the development of a commercialized economy. The ie, as the basic social unit, has been critical to an understanding of these problems.

A Marxist perspective, a major influence on Japanese historians of all eras, has also dominated thinking about the Tokugawa period. In the area of rural development, Furushima Toshio's work (1949) centering on agricultural technology has been most influential. His interest in the family was in its functions in supplying and organizing labor. He recognized a correspondence between family form and the type of agricultural technology. Hayama Teisaku (1981) notes a shift in perspective in the 1960's and 1970's, due to political demonstrations opposing the United States - Japan Security Treaty and to Japan's rapid economic growth. Many economic historians turned their attention to the analysis of Tokugawa governmental power and class conflict. Hayama argues for continued work on production as the economic base of any discussion of power relations and believes this approach will lead to a greater understanding of the peasant family. In his own work, he provides evidence from population and tax registers that family form, farm management, and income/social class are interrelated.

During the first century of the Tokugawa period, aggregate population grew rapidly. The economy also grew in response to improved agricultural productivity and development of commerce and manufacturing. What occurred in the latter part of the period remains the topic of heated debate among historians. Aggregate population appears to have been stable. Hanley and Yamamura (1977) argue that it continued to increase slightly through the entire period, but their assumptions and methods have been questioned. The stability of the population has supported Marxist scholars' contention that the economy of the last half of the Tokugawa period remained stagnant, resulting in increasingly poor living standards for the peasants. On the other hand, the non-Marxist see economic growth continuing, if at a slower pace, through the Tokugawa, leading to industrial take-off in the Meiji period, Hayami and others who have looked at the shūmonchō data conclude that although the aggregate population was stable, in fact there was a great deal of intra- and interregional movement. As population growth slowed or stopped in the more developed areas in the early 18th century, wage labor in commerce or manufacturing became an attractive alternative encouraging (the technically illegal) migration to urban centers, and creating a shortage of farm labor. This in turn raised the wages of farm laborers and servants. The Marxists argue that exploitation of the peasants, whether in agriculture or manufacturing, continued well into the Meiji period, providing the basis for Japan's industrialization (cf. Hane 1982).

Hanley and Yamamura (1977) take a strongly anti-Marxist position. They argue that as rational economic decision-makers, farmers chose to adjust the size of their families to the optimum level for their holdings. The average number of children for the four villages studied by analysis of shūmonchō was 3.5, a figure thought sufficient to guarantee an heir but not so many as to drain family resources. They found the proportion of population of working age to be high (60%), and believed that delayed marriage, large numbers of unmarried males, infanticide, and abortion kept fertility low. These practices reflected not extreme reactions to poverty as the Marxists believe, but rather attempts to improve the family's standard of living in a society of expanding opportunities. (I am not sure that these need to be mutually exclusive.) Mortality rates were also low, and even notorious famines did not have a long term impact on gradual population growth. Life expectancy at age two was about 40 years. Chapter 11 may be of particular interest since then the authors compare their own demographic case studies to the figures of Hayami, T. C. Smith, and others on the questions of life expectancy, crude birth and death rates, and the percentages of the population in working and in dependent age groups. Morris and Vlastos, in a critical review of this work (1980) point out problems with the authors' use of quantitative data, in regard to village data, particularly calculations of age at marriage and failure to adjust fertility and mortality figures for unrecorded infant deaths. But the reviewers agree with the description of economic development, and note the importance of the possibility that by the middle 18th century, Japanese farm families consciously limited fertility in exchange for a better lifestyle, an attitudinal change brought about by the greater availability of wage employment and increased ability to retain the profits of agricultural labor.

The individual most responsible for a shift in thinking about Tokugawa history based on demography is Hayami Akira. Although Sekiyama (1958) and Taeuber (1958) analyzed demographic data for this period, Hayami introduced the family reconstitution method, developed in European parish records studies, to the analysis of the shūmonchō. He and his co-workers of the "Keio University group" have analyzed in depth a number of villages in this way (see especially Hayami 1973a).

Hayami's various articles focus on different questions regarding different villages. In the village of Yokouchi, Hayami found a transition from population growth to stagnation due to decreased fertility, as seen in age specific marital fertility. He attributes this to the practice of family limitation. In Suwa County, which includes Yokouchi, there was a decline in mean household size from 7.04 in 1671 to 4.25 in 1870. By comparing areas of greater economic development with less developed areas within the county, he finds that the decrease in household size corresponds with the spread of a cash economy. Variables he considers in conjunction with mean household size include various family composition ratios (the highest correlation being with the number of married couples per household), fertility ratio; proportion of married males/female, mean age at marriage, and number of servants in the household. He finds that a decrease in mean household size parallels population growth, and suggests that large households with collateral kin and/or servants restrained population growth by inhibiting or delaying marriage. To restrain population growth with a small household system, positive birth control measures are needed (Hayami 1973, 1972).

In another article, Hayami investigates class differences in marriage and fertility in Mino Province. He distinguishes three classes of peasants based on their land-holdings, and finds an average of three years delay in marriage from class I (the largest land owners) to class III (the poorest group). This is likely to be due in part to women from poor families working for a period of time before marriage (see below) whereas class I women were less likely to work. It was not surprising, then, to find differences in fertility as well, since mean age at last birth did not differ. However, even with age of marriage controlled, poorer women had fewer children, which Hayami again attributes to the practice of birth control, more often among class III. Hayami also looks at marriage partners by class, and concludes that marriage was not a road for upward mobility among his sample (Hayami 1980b). (Moore 1970 and Yamamura 1985 conclude that adoption among the samurai also declined as an option for upward mobility.)

Hayami has also studied migration patterns for another area, the village of Nishijo. He is particularly interested in "temporary" labor migration, called dekasegi, of young, unmarried men and women. Over the period, there was decreased dekasegi to rural areas, and an increase to urban centers. Young people from tenant farming families were more likely to go away from home to work than were those from land-owning families, and they were likely to leave at an earlier age. Although dekasegi usually refers to a temporary migration for work, Hayami finds that only 27% of those leaving home ever return to Nishijo. For women, many married directly into another village; men faced an increased risk of death in the cities. (The mortality of women who did not go out on dekasegi was higher, presumably because they married earlier and thus faced the risks associated with childbearing.) Migration was thus an important factor in limiting population growth in the village; it also meant that as urban industry drew off labor power unequally by class, that tenant households had difficulty maintaining themselves over time (Hayami 1973, 1985).

Thomas C. Smith has provided another study of Tokugawa village life and demography in his analysis of the shumoncho from a village he calls Nakahara (Smith 1977). His data generally agree with the findings of Hayami and of Hanley and Yamamura. Where they diverge, as in relatively early marriage, Smith's data support Hayami's. He finds that larger land holdings correlate with larger household size and, like Hayami, believes that families consciously adjusted their fertility to the size of their holdings. But whereas Hayami leaves the matter there, Smith continues the argument. Based on the shumoncho analysis as well as the writings of contemporary officials and moralists, Smith convincingly argues that sex-selective infanticide played a major role in this process among all classes. Infanticide is mentioned by Hanley and Yamamura (1977) as well, but Smith shows that this method of fertility control was used to determine the sex sequence, spacing, and final number of children. Early in the period, sex selection was biased in favor of male babies, but later with the movement toward single-son inheritance and the development of light industry in which female labor was valuable, there were often attempts to balance the family sex ratio.

In a volume containing articles on both China and Japan, Hanley and Wolf (1985) summarize the research on family and demography in the Tokugawa period. They note that in Japan, as in Western Europe where the stem family also prevailed, age at marriage was high (although apparently adjusted to economic circumstances). Family planning was widely practiced both in the cities and in villages in Tokugawa Japan. Although abortion and infanticide were common among all social classes, the correlation between status and fertility is

negative, with samurai families having fewer children than the outcasts studied by Morris and Smith (1985). This suggests a changing social and economic
structure, as chances for samurai upward mobility for non-heirs decreased and
wage labor opportunities for lower classes increased. Wage labor often involved migration which contributed to low fertility in both rural and urban
areas due to the higher mortality and lower fertility of the migrants.

Tables 1 and 2 summarize the historical demographic work on the Tokugawa
period. Table 1, taken from Mosk (1981a) provides a statistical summary of
the above-mentioned studies. In Table 2, I list these and other studies,
grouped according to stages of the individual life cycle and related life
course transitions. Analysis of shūmonchō and other Tokugawa records continues both in Japan by Hayami and other demographic historians.

What does this research tell us about the family and the life course in
Tokugawa Japan? First, it views the rural and urban commoner populations as
rational decision-makers, capable of directing their own lives to some extent
within the limited (but expanding) economic opportunities and rigid political-
social structure of the Tokugawa period. Secondly, it offers demographic
evidence that neither the collaterally extended family nor the stem family can
be assumed to be operating in a given case, although it is likely that among
peasants, family form reflected differences in wealth (land ownership). Third-
ly, such family wealth differentials affected the individual life course in a
number of other ways as well, so that girls born into a tenant farm family
would be likely to marry later, bear fewer children, and have the experience
of living and working away from home before marriage, than would girls born
into families which owned a substantial amount of land. Fourthly, such poor
families would be less likely to continue over the generations according to
the ie ideal and more likely to be composed of a single married couple or even
a single adult householder.

Family Life Cycle in the Tokugawa Period. In 1959, Koyama Takashi wrote
an article entitled "Cyclical Change in Family Form" (translated and repub-
lished as Koyama 1981) which has been a major influence on sociological studies of the family (see Chapter 4). I would like to consider this work here
because, like the demographic studies above, Koyama also examines Tokugawa
peasant families using 19th-century shūmonchō data. Looking at a town in
Yamanashi prefecture, he finds that despite an extended family ideal, nearly
half of the 1556 families in the village were nuclear in form, with a much
greater proportion of three-generation families than in the 1920 census. In

TABLE 1
Measures of Fertility, Mortality and Population Increase for Selected Pre-Modern Japanese Villages

Population and date	Overall fertility, crude birth rate	Nuptiality* MAFMM	Nuptiality* MAFMF	Marital fertility† M	Marital fertility† m	Marital fertility† ALB	Birth intervals (years) average	Birth intervals (years) 0–1	Birth intervals (years) 1–2	Birth intervals (years) 2–3	Mortality Crude death rate	Mortality c_i Males	Mortality c_i Females	Natural rate of population increase
Kando-Shinden, c. 1800*	34.4	29.4	21.6	0.93	0.62	36.5	2.8	1.2	3.3	3.0	26.2	33.2	31.6	8.2
Yokouchi, before 1700**	35.3	26.0	18.8	0.67	−0.00	40.5	3.5	3.6	3.4	3.4	25.5	36.8	29.0	9.8
Yokouchi, after 1800**	22.2	28.0	21.7	0.46	0.36	33.6	3.3	2.0	4.5	3.8	18.9	n.a.	n.a.	3.3
Nakahara, eighteenth and nineteenth centuries	36.3	27.1	19.6	0.57	−0.10	37.5	3.6	2.6	4.4	3.3	26.6	46.1	50.8	9.7
Fujito, c. 1800	15.4	n.a.	22.9	n.a.	n.a.	34.1	3.6	n.a.	3.2	4.2	16.8	50.9	59.1	−1.4
Fukiage, c. 1683	31.0	n.a.	24.5	n.a.	n.a.	37.4	4.2	n.a.	4.7	4.1	15.9	n.a.	n.a.	15.1
Fukiage, c. 1860	19.4	n.a.	24.6	n.a.	n.a.	37.6	4.1	n.a.	4.2	4.1	22.2	n.a.	n.a.	−2.8

Sources:
(i) All figures, except crude birth rates, crude death rates, natural rate of population increase and c_is are from C. Mosk, 'Scandinavian Historical Demography: An International Perspective' (a paper presented to the panel on Scandinavian Social History at the Social Science History Association meetings, 4 November 1979), Table 3, pp. 12–17.
(ii) Crude birth rates, crude death rates and natural rate of population increases for Yokouchi and Nakahara and (c_is for Nakahara) are from T.C. Smith, *Nakahara: Family Farming and Population in a Japanese Village, 1717–1830*, Stanford, Stanford University Press, 1977, pp. 12, 40, 51.
(iii) Crude birth rate, crude death rate, natural rate of population increase and c_is for Fujito and Fukiage are from Susan B. Hanley and Kozo Yamamura, *Economic and Demographic Change in Preindustrial Japan, 1600–1868*, Princeton, Princeton University Press, 1977, pp. 211, 222.
(iv) c_i for Kando-Shinden from Akira Hayami, 'The Demographic Analysis of a Village in Tokugawa Japan: Kando-Shinden of Owari Province, 1778–1871', *Keio Economic Studies*, 5 (1968), p. 68.
(v) c_i for Yokouchi from Akira Hayami, *Kinsei Nōson no rekishi jinkō gakuteki kenkyū* (A Demographic Historical Study of the Tokugawa Village), Tokyo, 1973, p. 204.
* MAFMM = mean age at first marriage for males; MAFMF = mean age at first marriage for females.
† ALB = age of mother at last birth; 0–1 birth interval is from marriage to first birth. Birth intervals are in years and are all simple averages (means).
‡ Crude birth rate, crude death rate and natural rate of population increase are for 1838–42, the earliest period for which Hayami gives crude death rates. c_is is for persons who died between 1838 and 1869.
** Crude birth rate, crude death rate and natural rate of population increase for 'before 1700' relate to 1671–1700. For 'after 1800' they are for 1776–1871. c_is is for 1671–1725.
†† Crude birth rate, crude death rate and natural rate of population increase for 1800–1804. c_i is for 1800–05.
‡‡ Crude birth rate, crude death rate and natural rate of population increase for 'c. 1683' are for 1683–1700. For 'c. 1860' they are for 1854–60.

TABLE 2
References to Tokugawa Demographic Studies by Life Cycle Stage

Crude Birth and Death Rates (most of the studies calculate these)	Hanley and Yamamura (1977), Mosk (1981a) (see Table 1)
Dekasegi (leaving home to work)	Fruin (1973), Hanley (1973), Hayami (1973, 1985), Sasaki (1967, 1985), T.C. Smith (1969, 1977)
Marriage (age at first marriage, probability of marriage, bride's natal home, etc.) and Divorce	Hanley and Yamamura (1977), Hayami (1968a & b, 1973, 1980), Hayami and Uchida (1972), Kumagai (1983), Sasaki (1967, 1969, 1985), T.C. Smith (1977)
Childbearing (age at first birth, spacing, age specific fertility)	Hanley and Yamamura (1977), Hayami (1968a, 1973, 1980a & b, 1985), Hayami and Uchida (1972), Kito (1976), Morris and Smith (1985), Sasaki (1967, 1969), T.C. Smith (1977)
Population Control (infanticide, abortion, sex-selectivity, etc.)	Eng and T.C. Smith (1975-6), Hanley and Yamamura (1977), Hayami (1968a, 1973, 1980), T.C. Smith (1977)
Household Size	Hanley (1985) Hayami and Uchida (1972, 1973), Koyama (1981), Morris and Smith (1985), Nakane (1972), R. Smith (1972, 1973, 1985), T.C. Smith (1977)
Adoption	Hanley and Yamamura (1977), Hayami (1973), McMullen (1975), Moore (1970). T.C. Smith (1977)
Inheritance	Cornell (1981a & b, 1983), Hayami (1983) Ōishi (1981)

tracing transitions from one household type to another, he identifies a basic 23 - 24 year cycle, with family form most often following the movement from 1) household with one married couple and unmarried children; 2) household with two married couples and unmarried children of senior couple (senior generation as household head); 3) household with collateral relatives of head (same individuals as [2], but headship now with junior generation); 4) three-generation stem family; and back to [1] (see his Figure 2). By calculating a type of family dependency ratio, he further suggests a correlating cycle of family prosperity and decline. He concludes by warning that family form should not be taken as an indication of a cultural ideal. The nuclear family forms he finds in his data reflect stages of an extended family cycle, and not a conjugal ideal.

We also cannot assume that such a cycle was the norm throughout Tokugawa Japan. Taken together, the work of the demographic historians suggests differences by region, wealth, and social class. Robert Smith has investigated shūmonchō from four Tokugawa urban wards and finds differences from the reports from rural communities. More of his sample families are nuclear in form. But he emphasizes that the only ideal household in Japan is one that continues (succeeds!) and denies that there is an ideal type regarding household composition. It was the potential for a nuclear family to develop into a stem form which is important; it is not in itself imperfect, but is only a stage in a cycle. Most individuals lived some portion of their lives in extended (that is, non-nuclear) families and some portion in nuclear ones. He finds that the most common cycle for his sample is, unlike Koyama's, a movement from 1) nuclear family of one married couple and unmarried children; 2) two-generation stem with the junior male as head; 3) three-generation stem with middle generation male as head; and back to [1]. While some of this difference in findings may be due to flawed data (breaks in the records or small sample size), Smith also identifies demographic (individual life cycle) reasons for the succession of quite young males to headship. He raises important questions about the relation between changes in family form and the life cycles of individuals. (See R. Smith 1972, 1978, and 1985.)

Pre-War. There appears to be little quantitative work on the pre-war family, and that which has been done leaves room for multiple interpretations. Our interest in the pre-war period lies in its transitional nature, specifically in the relationship between the family and the rapidly developing industrial economy.

The person who seems to have addressed this question most directly is Fukushima Masao in his book Japanese Capitalism and the Ie System (1967). He first distinguishes between ie as a behavioral pattern in pre-Meiji Japan and the ie system. The latter, he argues, was a family organization consciously created by the Meiji ruling class to serve as the basis of a new political-economic system. The method of introducing this change was the koseki system (see above) and the civil code. The law of primogeniture, for example, he views as recognition by Meiji leaders of the need for capital accumulation and maintaining a reasonable scale of farm enterprise. He devotes a major portion of the book to a discussion of the zaibatsu's use of the ie ideology to amass capital and create modern enterprises, by keeping wages low and labor unrest suppressed (see also Fruin 1980, 1983). The family mediated between these industries and the workers, particularly by supplying cheap labor such as young women before marriage, whose labor provided supplemental family income. Production capital came primarily from light industry, which employed the majority of laborers, but many of these (such as the well-known textile industry) were viewed as "coming from the ie, and returning to the ie." Even for male industrial workers (who were also usually unmarried and quite young), the ie was considered the ultimate source of their welfare, so that low wages were possible as long as the ie was maintained. As security against unemployment, young workers kept up strong ties with their homes and during the Depression, many workers in fact did return there.

Fukushima also argues that the developing economy caused the reformulation of the family along "modern" lines. The modern, or conjugal family form appeared first in cities, historically, after World War I; by class, among workers and intelligensia. He suggests, however, that form and consciousness were not the same, and that workers probably did not feel themselves cut off from the ie as an ideational structure. The question of popular (as opposed to elite) attitudes toward the family in the Meiji period is approached by Arichi (1976) through analysis of opinions, incidents and advice from contemporary newspapers and magazines.

In the Meiji period, there were several areas in which households were unusually large, containing collateral relatives of the household head. (Fukushima analyzes the koseki records of one such region, Shirakawa, in his book.) Some people have interpreted these as representing the "traditional" family form, with the stem family as an intermediate stage (primarily during the Meiji period) on the road to modernization (see Koyama 1976). They base their argument on the breakdown of these feudal hold-overs as the cash economy and expanded labor marked encrouched on these relatively isolated, agriculturally poor areas. Nakane (1972), on the other hand, believes that areas such as Shirakawa represent anomolies created by the specific economic circumstances of a limited resource base that conformed to more usual patterns when the resource base was expanded in the Meiji period. The demographic evidence from the Tokugawa period (see above) suggests that at least for that period, small households averaging five people or less were most common (see table in Koyama 1976:279) and if anything, increased slightly in size in the late 19th and early 20th century.

Several other aspects of industrialization affecting family life are discussed by other authors. Saito (1973) examined labor migration patterns for Shizuoka prefecture from 1872 to 1920. He found that in cases where indigenous industry declined, out-migration might occur simultaneously with a local increase in wages in the modern sector. He speculates that this may be a result of earlier opportunities in indigenous industry which encouraged a high birth rate, creating excess population.

The demographic patterns associated with industrialization in Western Europe are not always found in prewar Japan. As in the West, the population grew rapidly in the early Meiji period (although Saito 1984 reminds us that the growth probably started earlier), followed by a decline in fertility. Mosk (1983) attempts to account for this transition in a mathematical model based on a "patriarchal stem family" and numerous demographic variables and measures of "modernization". He concludes that the fertility transition results from a breakdown of patriarchal control in an era of expanding educational opportunities and labor markets. (Oshima [1983] provides support for the relation between fertility decline and education in several Asian nations.) Mosk makes a number of questionable assumptions regarding actual behavior and how "closed" a system the preindustrial village actually was. (See reviews by Saito 1984 and Napier 1984.) Although his model is unconvincing because of this, he has assembled a large amount of data which can shed light on the changes in life course transitions accompanying industrialization (see also Mosk 1981b).

Several other demographic variables for prewar Japan do not conform to the usual pattern for industrializing countries. Mean age of marriage rose during industrialization (see Mosk 1981a). Divorce rates initially rose, but then declined dramatically (Kawashima and Steiner 1961, Goode 1963, Kumagai 1983). Illegitimacy decreased (Hayami 1980b) over the period, with urban areas showing these trends earliest. The family law code of prewar Japan undoubtedly played a role in these variations from the European experience, a subject taken up by family sociologists whose work is discussed in the next chapter.

SOCIOLOGICAL PERSPECTIVES ON FAMILY CHANGE

An Overview of Family Sociology in Japan

Approaches. Family sociologists in Japan trace the short history of their discipline to Toda Teizō who was active in the first third of the 20th century. Toda's contributions were both conceptual and methodological. He argued for the predominance of the individual over the group, a notion which drew reaction from contemporaries such as Suzuki who argued that an emphasis on the the individual was inappropriate to the Japanese case. Toda, having studied in the United States, first utilized statistical techniques to investigate family composition. He also made use of historical materials from the Tokugawa period (Morioka 1981a:iii).

Toda thus laid the groundwork for one of the major approaches to the family, the morphological approach. Within this approach, the main focus has been on the change in family size and composition from the stem or extended type to a nuclear type. The distinction between the two-generation family as a stage in the extended family cycle and the two-generation family as ideal cannot be directly inferred from the statistics. With the post-war influence of American sociology, methodology became more sophisticated. Koyama, et al. (1960) conducted a landmark study of family variation and change in the late 1950's in which they compared families in a mountain village, a suburban village, and a central Tokyo apartment complex. This study, which went beyond mere structural considerations, serves as a reliable base from which change can be measured. I will present results of this study in various sections to follow as appropriate to the topic being discussed.

The morphological approach also underlies the sense of problem of a more recent conference volume entitled The Household and Modern Family (Morioka and Yamane 1976). The authors' concern centers around the change from the ie to the "modern" conjugal family in Japan. Fuse's (1977) criticisms of this book apply to the morphological approach in general. It does not tie the family directly to the larger political and economic system. Moreover, it contains a premise of society as static and does not allow for non-statistical variation.

The second approach which can be seen in family studies of this period is that of Parsonian functionalism. These had a major impact on Japanese sociology in general after World War II. Examples in English are Koyano (1964) and

Yamane and Nonoyama (1967). Goode's work on industrialization and the family (Goode 1963) greatly influenced many Japanese family sociologists. He argues for the fit of the conjugal family with industrial society and for the eventual world-wide convergence of family form despite varying starting points and paths in countries around the world. Goode clearly states that his personal preference is for the freedom allowed in the "modern" system. Such functionalist assumptions underlie a number of other sub-approaches used in the mainstream of Japanese family sociology. An academic debate between Morioka Kiyomi and Yamamuro Shūhei focused on the interpretation of Toda's nuclear family theory, with Morioka arguing the functionality of the nuclear family in modern society while Yamamuro took the position that it was not universally so (Uno 1978b, Koyano 1976, Yamamuro 1981).

Mainstream family sociology in the 1970s approached the family from a developmental perspective. Suzuki was the forerunner of this approach when he applied ideas from Sorokin, Lively, and Cheyanov to develop a model of the family cycle of Japanese farm families. He was particularly interested in cycles of economic ease and hardship in relation to changes in family composition, but he did not allow for the influence of external factors in his model (Morioka 1964:8-11 in Kim translation). Morioka, as will be discussed later, is the chief successor to this tradition. Other uses of the developmental approach are Mochizuki's work on mate selection and Ishihara's on succession (see appropriate topics). Much of Koyama's work (e.g., 1960) has helped define this perspective. Although the life course perspective in the West focuses on the individual as social actor, these Japanese scholars working in the functionalist developmental tradition view the family as the central social unit.

Morioka (1981a:vi), suggests that another set of concerns also falls within the developmental perspective, although I would separate them under the functionalist umbrella. This is the study of the internal structure of the family, emphasizing roles and status relationships. The best-known work in this area has been done by Himeoka, et al. (1974), Kamiko and Masuda (1976), and Kamiko (1979). Koyama and his colleagues' studies of family roles (1967) and of parent-child relations (1973) and Fuse's work on dual career marriages (1967; in English, 1981) also exemplify this approach.

The perspectives I have just mentioned represent mainstream family sociology, but alternative approaches do exist. Given the prominent position of Marxist theory in Japanese intellectual thought, I have searched the available materials for examples in family sociology, but found only one reference to a book by Iida Tetsuya called, innocently enough, Family Sociology, published in 1976. The reference is a highly critical review of the book by Yamate Shigeru (1978). According to Yamate, the first part of Iida's book provides an historical perspective on the family, which Yamate claims remains unverified. Part 2 deals with family theory oriented toward social problems. Yamate finds his division of the post-war era into periods based on the United States-Japan Security Treaty renewals to be overly political, and argues that the analysis demands a greater inclusion of economic and sociocultural factors. I suspect that there are other Marxist family sociologists as well, but they seem to be uninfluential in their field, certainly as compared with the Marxist historians.

On the other hand, there appears to be a move away from functionalism in recent years. I have already mentioned Yamamuro Shūhei's disagreement with Morioka (for a later example of Yamamuro's writing, see Yamamuro 1973). A more recent debate has centered on a book entitled Rethinking the Nuclear Family by Kyoto University Southeast Asian scholars Tsubouchi and Maeda (1977). The authors investigated the Malaysian family and, finding the nuclear family concept not very useful, propose the notion of "family sphere" which draws on ideas of Leach and R.N. Adams. This conception of the family as an accumulation of dyadic relationships has been praised by Yamamuro (1978) but criticized by Oikawa in the Japanese Sociological Review. The authors, in turn, respond that Oikawa remains consciously or unconsciously bound by the concept of the family as a small group and thus ignores the basis of their argument (Tsubouchi and Maeda 1980). Their thinking may represent a movement toward interactional approaches generally, and/or is an indication of the contributions to Japanese family sociology that can be made through cross-cultural research.

I mention a possible trend toward interactional approaches because some scholars are openly advocating alternatives to the functionalist perspective. Meguro (Nojiri) uses exchange theory and social network analysis (1974b; 1977); Iwagami (1976) and others argue that analyses of case studies must supplement quantitative data; Masaoka (1981b) advocates a middle-range theory that recognizes both the structural and the behavioral aspects of the family. The work on conjugal power relations influenced by Blood was perhaps the first step in this direction.

Writing in the early 1980's, Morioka (1981a:ix-x) pointed to deficiencies in Japanese family sociology in four areas: 1) the lack of a cumulative process in research; 2) a lack of theory building; and 3) the need for better application of statistical methods; and 4) the lack of studies relating the transactions between the family and other social systems. In recent years, some Japanese family scholars have shown interest in the three-generational research methodology and results of Reuben Hill, and have become familiar with the work of Glen Elder and others involved in defining the life course approach. In 1980 the Japan Society for the Promotion of Science and the Social Science Research Council supported a planning meeting which resulted in series of conferences and seminars held from 1981 to 1984 on the family and the life course in Japan and the U.S. The Japanese researchers began a study in Shizuoka, Japan of the family life courses of middle-aged men (Morioka 1985) and several collaborative projects between Japanese and American researchers are currently in progress.

Research Topics. According to Morioka (1981a:x), there are now about 200 family sociologists. As the field has expanded, areas of interest have also increased so that mate selection, emotional relations in the family, the elderly and the family, and so on have been added to the traditional topics of husband-wife relations, parent-child-relations, retirement and succession, and family form and structure (Koyano 1976:42). There appears to be an emerging interest in women's studies (e.g., Meguro 1980) and a new look at possible sociological contributions to the solution of social problems which involve the family. (For example, see Aoi and Shōji 1980; Mochizuki and Motomura 1980; and Matsubara 1983.)

Although many family sociologists work on their own or within their own departments, three major research groups transcend institutional boundaries. The Kansai Family Studies Group was organized in the Kyoto-Osaka-Kobe area by Himeoka in the early 1950's. In 1955, Koyama founded a similar group in Tokyo called the Family Problems Study Group. These groups meet regularly for seminars and facilitate collaborative or joint research. Although their research topics sometimes overlap, the sense of problem of the two regional study groups differs. The Tokyo group tends to emphasize the morphological and family life cycle (developmental) approaches (due to the influence of Koyama [see Obituary by Morioka 1984c] and Morioka). The Kansai group appears to focus on internal family relations and role and power structures. Even when research topics are similar, members of each group refer largely to precedents in their own groups' research. Referencing of the work of the other group is weak except for "classics" such as Koyama's study (1960) or Kamiko and Masuda's study of the three-generation family (1976). A national conference, the Japanese Seminar on Family Sociology, which has convened yearly since 1968, has encouraged communication between the two regional groups as well as with other scholars.

Variables. A major problem in quantitive research is how to handle diversity. For the most part, the Japanese researchers break up their sample in ways familiar to American social scientists: by age (or generation), by social class (income, occupation), and by geography (urban vs. rural). Several of the concepts may require some explanation, however, in the Japanese context.

Respondents are most commonly broken into 10 year age groups, those in their 20's, 30's, 40's, and so on. Adulthood begins at age 20 both legally and in the public conception. Definitions of elderly vary, but researchers usually consider this stage to begin at either 60 or 65.

It has been common to talk about a "post-war generation", distinguishing those born and (especially) receiving their education after World War II from older cohorts who were educated under the old system. As I have already argued, there is validity to such a distinction based on the legal system and government-supported values. However, now that the post-war generation have their own children, the term becomes less useful. Generation is more usually used in sociology in the context of a single, usually co-residing, family. Morioka (1981c) has already provided us with a thoughtful review of relevant multigeneration studies, which have been limited to two generations of respondents.

How social classes are defined in terms of monetary income remains unclear in most studies. Occupational breakdowns are perhaps more interesting. The most common distinction is between those who are self-employed and those who are employees. The former includes owners of businesses, shops, etc. and most importantly, farmers who may be subdivided by size of farm or by proportion of income from farming. Employees can be subdivided into laborers (blue collar, not to be confused with day, or casual, laborers) and salarymen (white collar), or by size of industry. (A blue collar worker in a large corporation earns more and has much better benefits, including subsidized housing, pension plans, and greater job security than blue or white collar workers in small firms.) Many urban surveys specifically select locations that will reflect the subcultural variation between self-employed and salaryman households (cf.

Wimberly 1973). Many times, differences do appear along this dimension (see, for example, the section on co-residence, pp. 62-70).

The urban-rural difference is a critical one for many family sociologists, since behavioral and attitudinal change in urban areas, especially Tokyo, is considered predictive of national trends. Rural areas vary by region and are further divided by major mode of production (farming vs. fishing). Cities might mean one or more of the "six great cities" (Tokyo-Yokohama, Osaka, Nagoya, Kyoto, Kobe, Kitakyushu), a "regional city" (usually the prefectural capital of those not covered by the six largest cities, for example Okayama or Sapporo), and other cities (usually smaller, for example, Hirosaki, Himeji). The use of the term "suburban" differs from American notions of suburbia. It usually refers to a farming (or fishing) village on the outskirts of a metropolitan area which is often undergoing rapid change but may still rely largely on primary production. Narita, the site of Tokyo's international airport is an example. It should also be noted that all land in Japan is incorporated, so that the population of a city or town may include farming households. On the other hand, since four-fifths of farmers also hold non-agricultural jobs, the situation can become complex.

Resources. A "Summary Table of Post-War Japanese Survey Research on the Family" compiled by Yuzawa (1976) provides the most complete list of reports of original research through 1975, including national surveys by government agencies and the joint research projects of the study groups. For newer reports in journals, I suggest that materials in the following journals will prove most useful. The Japanese Sociological Review (Shakaigaku Hyōron) published by the Japan Sociological Association is the major journal in the field and often contains articles of or relevant to family sociologists. English abstracts appear together at the back of each issue. The Family Problems Research Group (the Tokyo-based group) began yearly publication in 1975 of the Annals of Family Studies (Kazoku Kenkyū Nenpō). Although this does not contain English abstracts, a translated Table of Contents is included. This journal publishes articles on original research and on theory, special symposia, and book reviews, and contains as well a section on "overseas news" and listings of theses and seminars. Studies in Family History (Kazoku Shi Kenkyū), described in the historical section of this paper, also contains relevant material. Another new journal includes interesting and important material for family sociology, the Japanese Journal of [Social] Gerontology

(Rōjin Shakai Kagaku). It is published yearly beginning in 1979 and includes English abstracts at the end of each article.

Change in Family Form

Household composition is changing in the direction of simpler forms, as Table 3 indicates. The most notable change has been an increase in the single person and conjugal forms, while the proportion of joint family households (including collateral relatives) has decreased. This change has occurred despite a decline in mortality over the period which would make three-generation households demographically more plausible (see Martin and Cutler 1983). In fact, in actual numbers, extended families (stem plus joint) have increased slightly. Yuzawa explains that the increase in single person house-holds can be attributed to an increase in quasi-households such as dormitories and boarding houses until 1965. After that time, the most important increase is among the elderly and young people (Yuzawa 1977b:13-15).

Corresponding to this change has been a decrease in mean household size, shown in Figure 1. In the 1920's, the mean household contained about 5 peo-ple, and this continued through the war and the post-war baby boom. Since then, the shrinkage in household size had been dramatic, to a mean household of about 3 people in the 1980's.

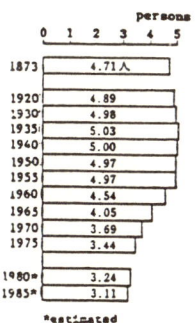

FIGURE 1
Change in Mean Household Size.

In Yuzawa 1977a:16

TABLE 3
Changes in Household Composition

		1920	1960	1965	1970	1975	1980
Nuclear Family Households	a. Couple only	10.3	8.3	9.9	11.0	12.5	13.1
	Couple & Child(ren)	38.3	43.4	45.4	46.1	45.7	44.2
	Father & Child(ren)		1.2	1.0	0.9	0.8	
	Mother & Child(ren)	5.4	7.3	6.3	5.5	4.9	6.0
	(subtotal)	54.0	60.2	62.6	63.5	63.9	63.3
Stem Family Households	b. Both Parents & Couple & Child(ren)		8.6	7.8			
	One Parent & Couple & Child(ren)	about 31	12.4	11.7			
	3-Generations including Collaterals		4.4	2.8			
	Other Stem Family		2.6	2.0			
	(subtotal)		28.0	24.3	25.4	22.2	20.7
	c. Households including other kin	about 8	6.7	5.0			
	d. Households including non-kin		0.4	0.4	0.4	0.2	0.2
	e. Single person households	5.9	4.7	7.8	10.8	13.7	15.8
Actual numbers in 10,000's	TOTAL	100.0	100.0	100.0	100.0	100.0	100.0
	Ordinary households	1,112	1,957	2,329	2,707	3,139	3,411
	Nuclear Family households (a)	601	1,178	1,458	1,719	2,007	2,159
	Extended Family households (b+c+d)	445	677	685	697	703	713
	Single person households (e)	66	102	186	291	429	539

From Yuzawa 1977b:14; 1980 figures from Japan Statistical Yearbook 1982.

Sociologists point to three major reasons for this change. 1) Couples are having fewer children. Crude fertility rates show the average number of children born to a woman was 5 in the 1920's, 4 in the 1930's and 1940's, 3 in 1950, and 2 from 1952 on. Social norms and the legal system of the post-war period support a small family ideal. 2) Neolocal residence at marriage had become the norm. Although non-successor children often establish their own homes at marriage under the _ie_ system, it is now common for all children to do so. 3) With industrialization and the rapid economic growth of the 1960's, people leave home for work-related reasons. Urbanization resulting from the shift from the primary to the tertiary sector has meant more people leaving home and moving to the more crowded living quarters of the cities (Yuzawa 1977b:17-18).

These trends in family composition influence family relations. The following sections review some of the research that has been done in this area.

Mate Selection and Marriage

Himeoka (e.g., 1983) has distinguished three outlooks on marriage: 1) the "communal" view in which marriage was seen to maintain and benefit the communal group; 2) the _ie_ view in which marriage was seen as a means to perpetuate and enrich the _ie_; and 3) the individualistic view in which independence and freedom of marriage is respected and marriage has value in itself. Marriage in Japanese society during the Meiji period is seen as moving from the first to the second principle. Since World War II, the historical trend has continued so that marriage now more often reflects the third principle (Mochizuki 1976:29).

The concept of a shift from a "communal" to an "ie" basis of marriage comes from ethnographic and legal evidence. Marriages among farmers and fishermen in the Tokugawa period were often based on self-selection rather than solely on the dictates of elders. Spouses generally came from within the village or from a nearby village. Families with significant power or wealth, however, would be more likely to arrange "appropriate" marriages for their children as in _samurai_ and merchant households. The values of the elite stressed premarital chastity and feminine obedience to parents and in-laws. To maintain political control, governmental permission was required for any marriage which crossed political or class boundaries. The Meiji government eliminated such restrictions and industrialization weakened the _dōzoku_ as a "communal" force on the lives of individuals. But rather than freeing individuals, toward Himeoka's third type of marriage, the government instead instituted the ie system, incorporating idealized samurai household and marital patterns into its family law. By instituting ie control over mate selection, the Meiji leaders actually imposed a more restrictive system on the majority of the population. (For a fascinating account of this change, see Smith and Wiswell 1982.)

Sociological researchers have more often focused on the change from the ie-oriented marriage to that based on individual preferences. The major categories (although these are often qualified, cf. Blood 1967) are arranged marriage (miai) and "love" marriage (renai). In the former, samurai daughters and obedient pre-war young women married a person introduced by a go-between and selected by her parents. The potential spouse was valued both for his family background and for his future, his ability to provide for their daughter. Parents generally tried to arrange the best possible situation for their daughter (based on their values) but were interested as well in the usefulness of the ties between the two families that were created by the marriage. Affection between the individuals was not considered an important factor in spouse selection. Renai marriage, on the other hand, reflects the "modern" values of individualism and free choice in marriage. When young people meet initially without parental involvement and decide on marriage later (often with parental consultations and the appointment of a ceremonial go-between), the marriage is considered a "love match".

Early sociological research related to mate selection was conducted by Toda, Koyama, and others in the 1920's and 1930's. Their concern was with the degree of class and geographical endogamy/exogamy. In particular, the geographical area from which a spouse might be chosen was hypothesized to expand with modernization. Results of koseki studies and local surveys were mixed, but generally supported the notion of a decrease in village-endogomous marriages. In the post-war period, however, Yasuda's studies failed to support the notion that horizons widen with modernization; rather as young people gained the freedom to choose their own spouses, propinquity became more marked. Yasuda also found that education played a more important role than occupational-class background in mate selection (Mochizuki 1976:24-27). Dore (1958), in his intensive study of a Tokyo ward, notes that the more recent the marriage, the more likely it was to be non-arranged. In his sample, most couples met at work, lived nearby, or were introduced by friends.

In Koyama's study of the family in a mountain village, a suburban farming village, and an urban apartment complex in the mid-1950's, survey results indicated a trend toward more "modern" mate selection in the urban setting. In both the mountain village and the apartment complex, the majority of respondents had met their spouses through introduction by a third person (52.3% and 55.4% respectively), less than 7% of the rural sample interacted freely with the potential spouse during the engagement period (compared with 35% of the urban sample) (Mochizuki 1972:58). By the time of a Ministry of Health and Welfare survey in 1966, marriages were about 50% miai and 50% renai based on subjective classification. In the more conservative rural areas, however, arranged marriages predominated (60%) while the ratio was reversed for the cities (40%).

Several government surveys in 1972 suggest rapid change has occurred since the time of Koyama's research. Table 4 compares responses to questions about interaction during engagement between Koyama's survey in 1957 and a Labor Ministry survey 15 years later. Although there remains a significant difference between urban and rural practices, the great increase in the proportion of respondents reporting free interaction is equally impressive. We might guess that the change is even greater than it looks since urbanization has left a greater proportion of older people in the countryside.

A 1972 survey from the Prime Minister's Office provides a breakdown by age for the question of arranged versus "love" marriages. Figure 2 indicates that miai marriages have decreased and renai marriages increased dramatically

TABLE 4
Engagement Period Experience of Married Women

		no inter-action	corre-sponded	met occasion-ally	inter-acted freely	other
1957	Mountain Village[a]	64.7%	5.7	14.8	6.7	8.1
1957	Apartment Complex[a]	25.1	10.4	23.8	35.1	5.6
1972	Rural[b]	34.6	2.7	35.4	25.7	1.6
1972	Apartment Complex[b]	5.1	3.7	26.8	63.5	0.9

a) from Koyama, et al., 1960
b) from Labor Ministry Survey

Yuzawa 1977a:25

in the 50 years or so represented by the survey sample. Nomura (1976b:57) looks at the same data as shown in Table 5. He shows significant differences at three points: 1) between pre- and post-war marriages; 2) between those who experienced sex-segregated junior and senior high school and those who experienced a co-educational era; and 3) between those born before and those born after World War II.

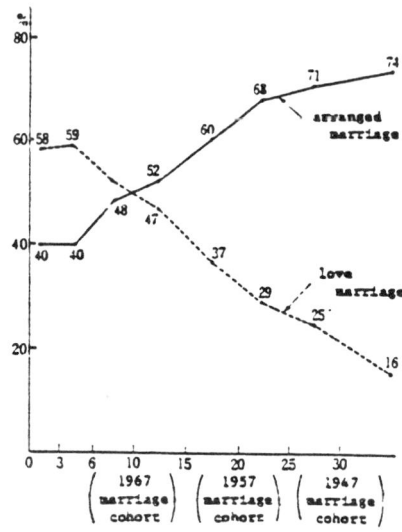

Years of Marriage

FIGURE 2
Type of Marriage by Age

From NHK, "The Image of Husbands and Wives," 1977
In Komobuchi 1981:41

TABLE 5
Type of Marriage by Age

age	20-24	25-29	30-34	35-39	40-44	45-49	50-54	55-59	60-69	70+
Proportion of renai marriages	71	55	41	34	24	17	11	9	8	6
			(3)		(2)		(1)			

(Nomura 1976b:57)

Mochizuki (1976:38-39) summarizes the results of the 1972 survey as follows: There is a clear trend from miai to renai, with a big change in the early 1960's paralleling the beginning of rapid economic growth. Geographical differences between urban and rural areas persist, with more renai in the cities. No differences were found by the woman's occupation (except agriculture), but the higher the educational level, the more likely a woman's marriage would be based on her own selection. Miai were more common in the upper and lower classes, but "love" marriages have undoubtedly become the norm for the vast majority of middle class Japanese.

Yuzawa (1977b) and Mochizuki (1972, 1976) point out that while the preference for "love" marriages has increased, lack of social institutions and a "dating culture" which allow young men and women to meet and decide about marriage have limited the meaning of renai in Japan. Using Koyama's survey as a base of "remnants of the traditional view of marriage" in which love was rarely considered an important criteria of marriage, studies by Yōda in 1972, Yuzawa in 1971, and others consistently find that personality, love, and health are reported to be the most important criteria in marriage decisions. More conservative values remain among the very highly educated and upper class (Mochizuki 1976:42-45).

As the form of marriage has become similar to that in the United States, comparative studies have become more viable. Mochizuki in particular has been utilizing concepts from American sociology. He devised a three-fold classification of ways of meeting a spouse: The first sphere is through family, relatives, etc.; the second sphere includes school and work; and the third is clubs and other outside interests. Cross-sectional data from the 1972 Labor Ministry Survey on the Status of Women suggests a strong shift from the first to the second sphere as a source for marital partners (Nomura 1976:58). Using a developmental task model, Mochizuki describes meeting, courtship, private understanding, sexual relations, and engagement for a small sample. He suggests that one major difference from the United States may be in the timing of these various stages. The entire period from meeting to marriage is short; the dating phase is particularly short and private understanding of a permanent commitment occurs early (Mochizuki 1981).

Wives and Husbands

Marriage. Marriage in pre-war Japan was characterized by its near universality and a low divorce rate. Through this period, the marriage rate ranged from 8 to 10 per 10,000 population. After a peak in the post-war years, it returned to previous levels in the 1950's and 1960's. However, the 1970's have revealed a marked decline (Komobuchi 1981:38) to 6.4 in 1983. From 1955 into the 1980's, 98% of women had experienced marriage by age 50. There has been a decline in the rate of unregistered (common-law) marriage from about 17% in the 1920's to 7% in 1940. (Marriages might not be registered until the birth of a child, for example.) National figures are not available for the post-war period, but a survey of Kyoto placed the rate for that city at 2.4%. Over 95% of marriages are now registered within a year of marriage as opposed to only 75% in 1950 (Yuzawa 1977b:25-27). Morgan, et al. (1984) found in their sample few exceptions to the normative sequence: marriage, conception, childbirth, but acceptance of premarital sexual relations as measured in opinion polls has increased (Mochizuki 1982).

The average age at first marriage of women, shown in Figure 3, has risen from 1920 to 1978. Men and women postponed marriage during the war years and married younger during the immediate post-war period.

Divorce. During the rapid industrialization of the pre-war period, divorce rates initially rose, and then declined steadily. Japanese sociologists have attempted to explain this deviation from the Euro-American experience by pointing out two quite different forms of divorce. Divorce based the modern family system increased with the breakdown of ie ideology, with industrialization and urbanization. Factors leading to a higher divorce rate might include increases in nuclearization of the family, renai marriage, independence of the family from the larger circle of relatives, and employment of married women; changes in attitudes toward marriage and divorce and changes in the functions of the family could also lead to more divorce.

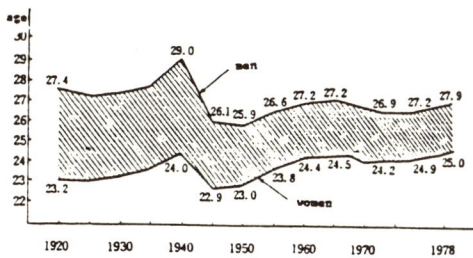

FIGURE 3
Change in Average Age at First Marriage and Age Difference of Spouses

From Ministry of Health and Welfare figures, 1978.
In Komobuchi 1981:39

On the other hand, the traditional form of divorce, usually based upon the desires of the husband's family, declined. This was due to behavioral changes resulting from pre-war education and the legal code, as evidenced by higher rates among farmers and lower rates among elite ie-oriented families. In fact, except for a peak immediately after World War II, the divorce rate continued to decline until the early 1960's. From a 1963 low of 0.73 per 10,000 population, the rate has begun to rise gradually to 1.22 in 1980 (Yuzawa 1977b:35-36; Kōsei Tōkei Kyōkai 1982:81). Tokuoka (1981:91) suggests that this is still low by international standards due to the Japanese cultural emphasis on maintaining good human relations. Reasons for divorce have also changed. Under the current system, 90% of people select "divorce by mutual agreement" in which no reason for the divorce need be given. However, the available data suggest a shift in importance from family problems to individual or conjugal problems and from social/economic factors to personal and psychological ones (Yuzawa 1977b:36).

Masuda (1981:71-72) points out a change of particular interest in life course studies. According to 1978 Ministry of Health and Welfare statistics, divorce in the first five years of marriage is decreasing, while divorce after five years up to ten years of marriage is increasing. Thus divorce cases are increasingly involving children. The proportion of middle-age and older divorces has increased from 19.7% in 1955 to 30.7% in 1978. In the Meiji family system, children automatically remained with their father's family. From the early 1960's, courts have more often awarded custody of a single child to the mother and given custody of two children to the mother from the late 1960's. In 1974, fathers retained custody in over 35% of the cases (Yuzawa 1977b:38).

Roles, Authority, and Power. Claiming that the image of husband and wife as a couple is weak in Japan, Masuda quotes three Japanese sayings to characterize the traditional husband-wife relationship. "A bride three years without children departs" expresses the emphasis on the parental role over the conjugal one. A traditional husband demanded "food, bath, and bed." Different behavior was expected of males and females from childhood, both reflecting and creating social distance and communication barriers between the sexes. The extremely strong sex role differentiation was expressed in the words, "A man takes care of the outside, a woman takes care of the inside" (Masuda 1981:55). In a 1949 public opinion poll, 62% of the respondents agreed that "A man should run the home and his wife should obey." However, four years later, only 44% agreed with the same statement (Yuzawa 1977b:29).

Although it may be differently interpreted from the old saying, a sharp sex role differentiation continues. Results of a 1962 survey of conjugal role expectations by Yuzawa, et al. indicated little variation by family form, age, or husband's occupations. Husbands most desired wives with whom they could talk and who exerted themselves to foster their children's education. Wives desired husbands who worked hard and who were not violent. They were least interested in having a husband who drank or one who helped with the housework; husbands were uninterested in economic assistance from their wives. A strong role differentiation in which the husband is the breadwinner and the wife the home manager and child-rearer is reflected in a 1972 public opinion poll, a 1972 study by Maruyama Naoko (Yuzawa 1977b:32-34), and a 1977 NHK Survey (Masuda 1981:58). The Economic Planning Agency, moreover, reported that its 1979 survey indicated that the strongest images of differentiated sex roles were among the younger generation. In fact, the NHK survey found that over 50% of women in all occupational categories "hold the pursestrings" (85% in salaryman families) as managers of the home; a Nihon Keizei Shimbun questionnaire survey found that 22% of men help with laundry, 34% with cooking, and 18% with care of children (Masuda 1981:64-65), tasks considered within the women's domain. A 1985 opinion poll found that 76% of its respondents in Japan (as opposed to 37% of American respondents) believe that husbands should make the final decision when husband and wife disagree (Sōrifu Hōkokushitsu 1981).

Despite continued sex role differentiation, Masuda sees a trend toward increased equality of power. Using Blood's typology to analyze data from a 1963 study in Kobe, Masuda concluded that the majority of couples were of the autonomic type, that is, the husband and wife each make independent decisions in their own spheres of authority. The lower the educational level of the husband, the less power he had in the family. A wife's power in the home increased with years of marriage. Himeoka reported class differences in family power structure from a study in Kyoto in 1966. The husband-dominant type was more frequent in upper class families, the wife-dominant in lower class homes, and the trend toward equality was strongest in the middle class (Masuda 1972:94-95). Of the respondents to a recent government survey, 63% of men and 75% of women who said they had someone they could turn to for advice said that person was their spouse (Sōrifu Hōkokushitsu 1985).

Masuda believes that greater equality and the increased importance of conjugal love among couples born in the post-war period may result from coeducation, greater education for women, renai marriages, and a decreased age difference between spouses. Journalists refer to this as the "new family." Masuda also notes (although I doubt that he is referring to Japan specifically) other "anti-familism" trends represented by couples living together with no intention of marrying, increased recognition of homosexual marriages, and religious and ideological communes (Masuda 1981:58-60). Kumagai and O'Donoghue (1978) have investigated conjugal violence in Japanese and American families, but fail to establish a positive correlation between such violence and power relations within the family.

The Lengthening of the Conjugal Period. Masuda points out that the husband-wife relationship has increased in importance not only because of new values and forms of marriage. From a life cycle perspective, it has increased in importance because the length of time the husband and wife spend as a "couple household" has increased dramatically. Even with delayed marriage due to higher education, a greatly lengthened life span together with a shortened period of child-rearing due to fewer births has meant a significant period in middle and old age in which the conjugal relationship is primary. A Health and Welfare White Paper of 1976 on changes in women's life cycle compares figures from 1940 and 1972. In 1940, the average length of marriage (both spouses alive) was 22 years, compared to 44 years in 1972. Moreover, with larger families, the 22 years would have corresponded with the span of child-rearing. In 1972, a couple had an estimated 15 years together after the last child married (Masuda 1981:68). These figures, however, are based on life expectancy at birth; the change would not be as drastic if life expectancy at age of marriage were used.

Working Wives. Studies by Fuse (see Fuse 1981) and Sato conclude that the wife's employment alters the conjugal relationship so that cooperative decision-making becomes more common and the sex role division of labor shifts (Masuda 1972:96; see also Kamiko 1979). The larger increase in employment of married women that accompanied economic growth in the 1960's and 1970's is likely to have a major impact on the Japanese family. It also seems that the study of working women has become a popular subject of inquiry in recent years (cf. Takahashi 1976, Iga 1978, Japan Institute of Labor 1981). Meguro (1980) has even argued a need for "women's studies" from a radical feminist perspective (see Ishihara's [1981c] review).

Female participation in the labor force declined from 56.7% in 1955 to a low of 45.7% in 1975. From 1976, there has been an upward trend, with the 1980 rate at 47.6%. These percentages hide an increase in real numbers from 17,400,000 women working in 1955 to 21,850,000 in 1980. In addition, there has been a shift away from family workers to employees, with the proportion of women employed outside the home rising from 31.2% in 1955 to 63.2% of all working women in 1980 (Japan Institute of Labor 1981:7).

The most important change in female employment for our purposes has been that in the past, young and unmarried women constituted the majority of the female labor force, with less than 20% aged 40 and over. In 1980, middle-aged women constituted 41.5% of the female labor force. In 1949, the average age of female workers was 23.8; in 1979 it was 34.8 years. Figure 4 shows that the proportion of married to unmarried working women has nearly reversed from 1960 to 1980 (Japan Institute of Labor 1981:6-10).

Yuzawa summarizes the effects of this change on the family as follows: 1) Working wives do get a little more help with the housework than their non-working counterparts, but still suffer from a lack of time. They average 4 hours less per day on household tasks than non-working wives. 2) Working wives have a greater input into major family decisions than non-working wives, especially financial decisions. Their family decision-making approaches Blood's "cooperative type". However, this also means decreased autonomy in daily matters as their husbands have more say in such decisions. 3) Outside employment increases the wife's stress. 4) There is mixed evidence regarding the effects of women's employment on their children. There are both positive and negative effects on the women themselves. However, Yuzawa suggests that continuing social prejudice against married women's employment has limited the number of women who have their own work careers (21% in 1975). A 1972 survey reports that 63% of women and 46% of men believe it is all right for women to work after marriage (Yuzawa 1977b:33-34).

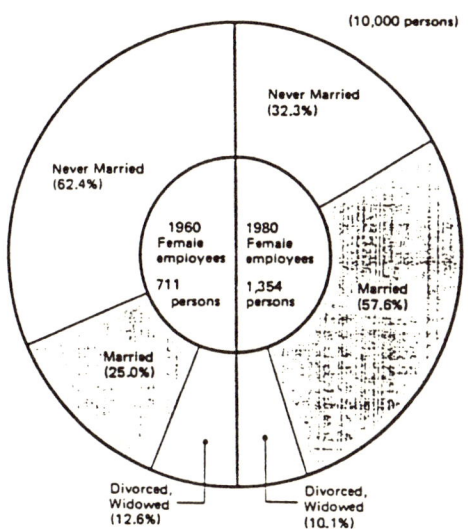

(10,000 persons)

Never Married
(32.3%)

Never Married
(62.4%)

| 1960 Female employees | 1980 Female employees |
| 711 persons | 1,354 persons |

Married
(57.6%)

Married
(25.0%)

Divorced, Widowed
(12.6%)

Divorced, Widowed
(10.1%)

Source: Prime Minister's Office: *Population Census* (1960)
Prime Minister's Office: *Labour Force Survey* (1980)

FIGURE 4
Female Employees by Marital Status

In Japan Institute of Labor 1981:10.

What does this mean for the individual woman's life course? I have already mentioned the lengthened conjugal period that results from smaller families and increased longevity. The change from 1940 to 1979 is shown graph-
ically in Figure 5. Many women are now returning to the labor market during
the "extra" middle years. The most common pattern is for a woman to work for
several years after completion of her education. After taking time out for
child-rearing, she returns to the labor market, although her income remains
supplementary in nature. Part-time employment is often selected by working
wives (Japan Institute of Labor 1981:5,7,11). Given that the average age at
marrage is 25 (Komobuchi 1981:39) and the average age for returning to work is
35 (Japan Institute of Labor 1981:7), the "average" working woman becomes a
full-time housewife for approximately 10 years. (For data on Japanese working
women, see Cook & Hayashi 1980 and Robins-Mawry 1983.) Ethnographic accounts
provide life course analysts a different type of data on the women behind the
statistics (for example, Bernstein 1981; Plath 1980; T. Lebra 1981; Vogel

1978; Long 1986; Pharr 1981; and articles in J. Lebra 1976 and Plath 1975 and 1983). In particular, T. Lebra (1984) offers us intimate views of the familial and work careers of contemporary Japanese women, and comments on both the cultural meanings of their experiences and on the effects of life course and historical changes in women's roles.

Parents and Children

In this section, I will review Japanese studies of parents and their young and adolescent children. I will deal with older parents and their adult children in later sections.

Family Planning. Intertwined as both cause and effect with changes in parent-child relations has been the universalization of family planning and the decrease in fertility. The demographic transition began in the pre-war period. However, during the war, the government encouraged a high birthrate. This policy has changed in the post-war period, and following the post-war baby boom, fertility has continued to decline. Limitation of family size by contraception and induced abortion has become nearly universal. Yuzawa (1977b:40) estimates that about 70% of birth limitations in the early 1950's were by induced abortion, but by 1965, 70% were by contraceptives. Coleman (1983) states that the most common contracepting methods were condom, rhythm, and other "traditional" methods, in contrast to sterilization, oral contraceptives, and IUD use. He quotes Mainichi Newspaper surveys which showed an increase in contraceptive practice from 40% in 1959 to 60% in 1979, but the proportion of contracepting couples who relied on condoms actually increased from 79% in 1977 to 82% in 1979.

Limiting family size was primarily motivated by a desire for a higher standard of living in the 1950's (and earlier), but the primary motivation from the 1960's has been to provide higher education for children (Yuzawa 1977b:40, Yamamura and Hanley 1975). The result has been not only a decrease in average number of children per family to less than 2 (Table 6), but also the "bunching" of births in the woman's late 20's to assure that the children can complete their education before her husband's retirement. (See also Coleman 1983:119-121; Morgan et al. 1984.) Looking at aggregate data, Ohbuchi (1976) agrees that the fertility decline after the late 1950's is of a different nature than the earlier trend from pre-war days, and he concludes that the effects of timing are particularly strong. As recently as 1973, public opinion surveys reported that while couples were having an average of two children, the ideal remained at three, and some people predicted an increase in

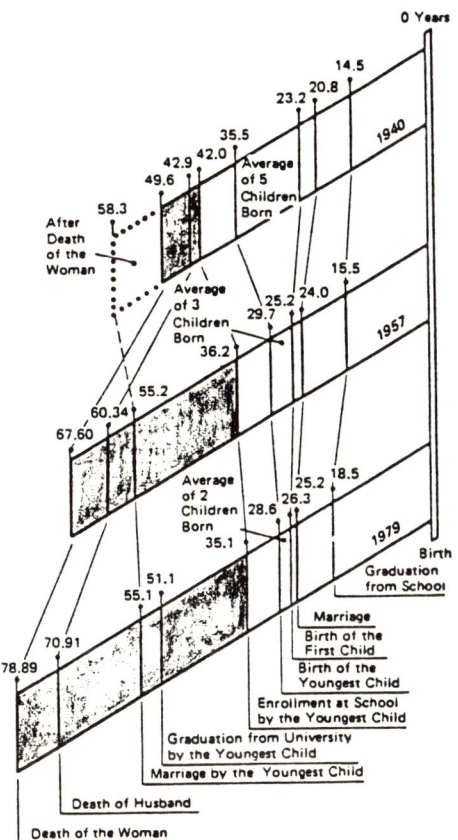

Source: Ministry of Health and Welfare: *Vital Statistics, Sim-plified Life Expectancy Chart* and *Survey on Child-bearing Capacity.*
Ministry of Education, Science and Culture: *School Basic Statistics.*

Note: This model is based on average figures for each life stage.

FIGURE 5
Japanese Women's Model Life Cycle

In Japan Institute of Labor 1981:5.

fertility as the economic situation improved. Perhaps because it did not in 1973, by 1975, the ideal came to agree with the reality (Yuzawa 1977b:40).

Although fertility continued to decline in the late 1970's, Atoh (1981) believes that this reflects not a further alteration of the ideal, but rather the rise in the mean age at marriage for both sexes which is due in part to the increasing proportion of women receiving higher education.

TABLE 6
Change in Average Number of Children Per Family

	1920	1930	1940	1947	1952	1957	1970	1978*
Average Number of Children	5.24	4.71	4.11	4.52	3.00	2.03	2.14	1.79

* Estimated

In Yuzawa 1977:41.

Fewer and "bunched" births have altered the life cycle of women so that they have a longer period when their mothering services decrease in importance, encouraging increased labor force participation and possibly altering the family power structure. Women's return to work may be motivated by the same desire as family planning: to allow for the higher education of the children by increasing family income. (It is not only tuition and maintenance costs that are of concern; expensive special preparatory classes after school and private tutoring during high school are considered to give a competitive edge in admissions to the best colleges and universities.) Yuzawa (1977b:41) also suggests that with fewer children, the mother can devote more attention to each, creating closer mother-child ties and a tendency toward overprotectiveness.

Child-Rearing. Another important group of studies I wish to discuss concerns what the Japanese call shitsuke. Kenkyūsha's New Japanese-English Dictionary translates shitsuke as "teaching manners; breeding, upbringing; training, discipline." Since shitsuke covers a broad range of English words, and since it can be "good" or "bad", I have usually translated it as "child-rearing." I do want to point out, however, that the nuances of shitsuke can range from "socialization" to "disciplining", depending on the context. (See also Makino's discussion, 1970:141-142.)

Yuzawa (1977b:42-44) characterizes changes in child-rearing patterns as follows: for most pre-war families, concern with making a living and numerous children meant a relatively free, natural, unplanned upbringing for the children. Grandparents and older sisters often shared in the childcare responsibility. In a 1939 rural survey, Aoki found that most infants and babies slept with their mothers (94% of newborns, 59% of babies), that weaning was gradual (86%), that favorite snacks were given between meals (78%), that babies were constantly held or carried on the back (64%), and that children were allowed to make as much of a mess as they desired (62%). In rural areas, a notion that children are "before age 7, among the gods" led to lenient child-rearing. However, from age 7, discipline suddenly became strict, and occupational training was begun in earnest by requiring the child's help in work. According to a study by Tokuoka, adolescents were trained to be hard working, frugal, and rank-conscious, and to perpetuate the ie and revere its ancestors. They mastered form rather than content by watching and imitating. Undesirable behavior was punished with ridicule, ostracism, withholding of food, or corporal punishment (Yuzawa 1977b:43).

Government opinion polls in the 1980's have found that the majority of people surveyed think that strict disciplining of children is necessary (69%, but the American response was 78%). They agree with the statement that lax child-rearing is the cause of juvenile delinquency (64%) (Sōrifu Hōkokushitsu 1981, 1982). However, in contrast to the pre-war period, many mothers have now become solely responsible for the children's care and upbringing. In 1964, only 55% of children in a survey by the Family Problems Research Association ate dinner with their fathers. As hours of employment lengthened, the children's relationship with their father weakened, and the father became less available as a role model. (See Aldous and Kamiko [1972] for a cross-national perspective on father-absence; their discussion does not, however, include fathers who live with their wives and children but are rarely home.) With increasing nuclearization of the family, grandparents less often participate in child care, and even in three-generation families, shitsuke has increasingly come to be seen as something in which the older generation should not get involved. Standards and values have changed and so, although most parents respond that they rely on their own childhood experiences as a guide in handling their children, they feel a lack of confidence about child-rearing (Yuzawa 1977b:43-44). Hosoda (1976) found that working mothers (except those in the managerial, professional, and technical categories), those in conjugal families, and those whose husbands were laborers had the most self-doubts. Hosoda notes, however, that the variables cluster, so that the mothers most self-confident about their child-rearing are likely to have self-employed husbands, be living with her in-laws, and have sufficient family income to not be working outside the home. The major studies of child-rearing practices are the above mentioned survey by the Family Problems Research Association (cf. Koyama 1973; see also Aoi 1970 for a detailed English language report) and a survey of junior high school students and their parents by Himeoka, et al. (1974).

Despite the changes that have occurred in child-rearing, Caudill's comparative work of the 1960's indicates that caretaking behavior in urban middle class families Japanese families differs from that in American middle class urban families. Detailed observations showed that the time spent for necessities such as sleeping, clothing, bathing, and diapering was similar, but by the age of three to four months, mothers and infants in the two societies had quite different interactive patterns. Most conspicuous was the greater amount of verbal interaction between American mothers and infants and more cuddling, carrying, and holding on the part of Japanese mothers (Caudill and Weinstein 1969). Interestingly, the pattern in self-employed Japanese households was more similar to the American, leading Matsuo (1981:123-4) to suggest that change will lead to divergence from the American pattern (on the assumption that the self-employed represent a conservative element in Japanese society).

The differences in social values associated with pre-war and with post-war society, along with visible signs of adolescent rebellion from blue jeans to student revolts, has led to discussion in the media of a generation gap. Several studies have investigated this gap but conclude that it is small. The 1977 Youth Consciousness Survey asked young people in a number of countries if, in recent years, they had had a disagreement with their parents about which they felt unable to compromise. Sixteen percent of Japanese youth responded affirmatively, as opposed to 35% in West Germany, 33% in Switzerland, 29% in England, 24% in the United States, and 13% in Sweden. The content of the disagreement in Japan, moreover, was less likely to be about one's outlook on life, and more likely to concern studies. Japanese young people and those of Western Europe and the United States disagree with their parents to a similar extent regarding daily habits such as hair style, dress, time for returning home, etc. (Nomura 1981:163).

Lebra studied a sample of adults and young people in a provincial city to explore the gap in morality between the pre-war and the post-war generation. Her findings strongly support neither generational continuity nor discontinuity, but she suggests that while young people may resist "traditional morality", they are not alienated from moral values in general. Moreover, what alienentation there is does not apply to the family even regarding such issues as filial piety. The majority moral orientations were shared by the generations; divergence (which may be due to life cycle stage) appeared primarily in minority responses (Lebra 1974).

Lebra's finding that the generation gap does not apply to the family is supported by international survey results on attitudes toward parents living with adult children. Differences between Japan and the other countries were much greater than between the generations, as Figure 6 indicates (Nomura 1981:164). Within Japan, Himeoka found that adolescents' sense of belonging in the home was greatest in husband-dominant families in a city (followed by equal-type) and in equal-type families in a rural area (followed by husband-dominant) (Masuda 1972:97-8). Recent popular and scholarly interest has focused on the apparently new phenomenon of parent-abuse by "good" adolescents (Kumagai 1981, Kawai 1981) and on school refusal syndrome (Lock 1986). Parent-child relations seem to be increasingly viewed as problematical (at a social, if not individual, level) (e.g., Yamamura 1983). Ambivalence and disagreement about the best way to raise children may be reflected in the responses to a survey question: "Regarding relations between parents and young children, do you think there is not enough contact or that parent-child relations are too close ('thick')?" Twenty-two percent of respondents chose "not enough contact"; 32% said relations are too close; 37% replied they were unable to choose between the responses; and 9% responded "Don't Know."

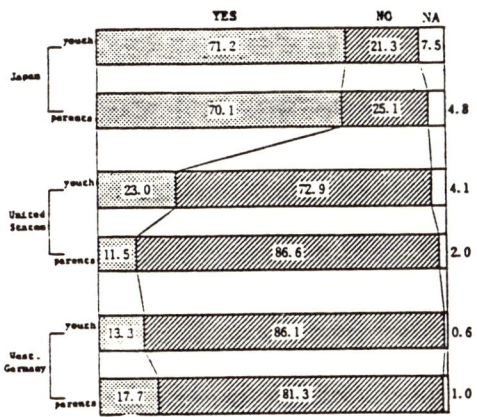

FIGURE 6
Is it Best for Parents to Live with Their Adult Children?

From Prime Minister's Office Survey "Young People's Sense of Rules," 1975.
In Nomura 1981:164.

Succession

The study of succession constitutes a relatively distinct subfield which involves legal scholars as well as sociologists. Most of the work on succession and retirement practices consists of case studies of particular villages or regions and focuses exclusively on farm households. The concern with succession relates directly to the ie model. Retirement and succession were the mechanisms of intergenerational continuity of the ie, involving the transfer of role authority and responsibilities from father to son and from mother to daughter-in-law. Research documents local variation in retirement and succession practices (see Tsuchida 1976, Okamura 1976, Takai and Nakao 1977, Yōda and Toshitani 1977 for Japanese-language reviews of this data), including age, the building of separate retirement cottages, the type and extent of the retiree's participation in production, and so forth. The major point remains that, although many successions occurred at the death of the household head, succession before the death of the elder generation of the household occurred frequently and there existed a specific role of "retiree" in the ie system. The Japanese term for retirement is inkyō; retirees were called inkyō-sama, "sama" being an honorific form of address.

A report of Ishihara's excellent study of succession to household headship in two nearby hamlets from 1965 to 1975 is available in English (Ishihara 1981a). Ishihara makes the important point that the transfer of the headship is a gradual process; this process now begins and ends later in the life cycle than in the pre-war period due especially to increased longevity, but also to conservative reactions to the post-war reforms and to increasing urbanization (and accompaning abandonment of farming). These trends have been found in other locations in Japan as well (e.g., Yōda and Toshitani 1977, Tsuchida 1976). Yet the system of retirement/succession seems to remain relatively intact for farm households. As Ishihara (1981a:360) notes, the last factor, abandonment of farming, is likely to have the greatest impact on retirement and succession in the near future.

Retirement for the majority of the Japanese population has become separate from the question of succession. About two-thirds of Japanese companies, and all of the largest ones, have a mandatory retirement system. Maeda (1978) estimates that this applies to over half the Japanese work force. Mandatory retirement requires a different sort of planning for one's life, since the flexibility and gradual nature of the role transition no longer applies. An additional problem is that the mandatory retirement age in most organizations is low relative to that in other industrialized countries. Fifty-five had been the standard retirement age, but as the government encountered increased pressure on its social security system, it has raised the mandatory retirement age for civil servants to 60 and pressured the private sector to respond similarly. Retirement age for workers with mandatory retirement now ranges from 55 to over 60.

Companies rarely have pension plans for retiring workers, but rather give a lump sum payment at retirement. Eligibility for government pensions (social security) begins at age 60. Maeda (1978:54) points out that if a man marries in his late 20's and his last child is born when he is in his mid- to late 30's, that child will still be in high school or college when he reaches his mid-50's. Because of financial need as well as a desire to continue working (see Kii 1979), a variety of employment situations arise. Mandatory retirement may not apply to a few people such as executives of corporations. People in other jobs who are difficult to replace may be allowed to continue working, though often with reduced pay and benefits. More often, a worker must find another job to support his family, a job that usually carries less prestige and lower pay than his pre-retirement job. Large companies may offer such opportunities in their own or in subsidiary companies to well regarded workers. The government has continued to pressure companies to extend their mandatory retirement age.

Inheritance. Under the ie system, the corporate property of the ie was not only the means of livelihood of the ie members, but also the means of and partial rationale for ie continuity across the generations. Thus, a single heir (couple) inherited, and in turn was obligated to preserve and if possible enrich the corporate estate. Under the post-war constitution, parental property is to be divided equally among all children of both sexes. Farmland, however, came to be exempted from this requirement so that production would not be hurt by splintering already small farms.

But what of the vast majority of Japanese who live in cities and towns? First, while all of the materials I have reviewed discuss succession and inheritance in relation to rural areas, there exist some urban households whose livelihood depends upon an investment in property and who see it as desirable to pass on this property to succeeding generations. These include family-run business owners such as shop keepers, restaurant owners, and pharmacists, dentists, and physicians in private practice. Private practitioners in Kyoto are statistically showing an increased willingness to sell a practice outright at the death or retirement of the physician, but my own work among physicians suggests that finding a successor still appears to be the most desirable solution (See Long 1980, Chapter 6).

Arichi, a legal scholar, discusses property inheritance in a recent article in Studies in Family History (1981). He quotes a 1980 government survey of people 60 years and older which found that a majority of older people (68.6%) thought of their real estate as "family property" to be passed on to the children. Over three-fourths of the respondents supported the concept of joint property (husband-wife) even when the wife did not contribute directly to the family income. The most interesting finding is that more than 30 years after legal provision for equal inheritance, only 12% of people over 60 supported it, while 43% supported inheritance by the eldest son. Support or unequal "compensatory" inheritance has increased from earlier surveys. In "compensatory" inheritance, the parent leaves all or a larger share of the property to the child (not necessarily the eldest male) who cares for him/her in old age. Thirty-nine percent of the 1980 respondents favored this form of inheritance. As early as 1968, over half of the respondents in one survey agreed that it was acceptable to not give to non-caretaker children. Arichi believes "compensatory" inheritance to be an emerging new consensus led by urban, educated salarymen and housewives (Table 7), a consensus which brings together the policy areas of inheritance law and old age support.

Arichi also has an interest in a life course perspective. He observes that with people dying at older ages, inheritance of property such as real estate becomes relatively meaningless for their children who, probably in their 50's, are by then preparing for their own retirement. It is their grandchildren who are beginning their own families, saving to buy a home, etc. for whom the inheritance of property would be most beneficial.

Adoption. In the traditional system, adoption was often the means of securing a successor. As the proportion of farm households has decreased, it is not surprising that the number of adoptions has decreased (102,000 cases in 1952 to 87,000 cases in 1974). Adult heirs (yōshi) may be adopted without court permission. Commonly, son-in-laws, this form of adoption has remained at about the same level from 1952 to 1975. Adoption of minor children, however, has decreased from 31.3% to only 7.7% of all adoptions, primarily because of decreased fertility, and a decrease in the number of orphans, single-parent children, and illegitimate children. Parent's motivation in adopting

TABLE 7
Support for "Compensatory" Inheritance among Persons 60 Years and Older

All respondents	39.1%
Men	34.0
Women	46.5
Primary & junior high school graduates	33.1
Graduates of schools of higher education	40.8
Living with descendents	32.7
Living separately from descendents	40.9
Employees	41.0
Self-employed, managers	36.9
Farmers	35.0
Housewives	44.9
Rural	32.7
Urban (large cities)	36.7

From Arichi 1981

minor children has changed little. Seventy to eighty percent adopt because they have no child of ther own; few parents give family continuity as their reason for adopting. Since adoptive parents have been married an average of 7-10 years, most are in their late 30's or early 40's when adoption takes place. Interestingly, more girls than boys are adopted (about a 55:45 female: male ratio since 1952), supporting the notion that questions of adoption and of succession have become quite distinct (although a son-in-law, married to the adopted daughter, might still become a successor). Over half of the adoptions of minor children are of blood relatives, usually a niece or nephew, accounting for the fact that 70% of adoptees have both parents alive and only 15% were illegitimate births (Yuzawa 1977b:45-47).

TABLE 8
Attitudes Toward Adoption

"Do you think that when there are no children, an ie should be continued by adopting a yōshi even if the child is unrelated by blood? Or do you think continuation would be unnecessary?"

Year	Continue	Would not continue
1953	73%	16%
1958	63	21
1963	51	32
1968	43	41

In Kamiko 1981:17

The Elderly and Their Family Relations

The Demographic Background. The lengthened life span of the Japanese has been a causative factor in many of the changes discussed in this volume. Table 9 indicates that the average life expectancy at birth has increased by about 30 years from the turn of the century. As Yuzawa (1977a:176) points out, however, the much lower life expectancies of the earlier years were due to infant and child mortality, and to deaths of young adults from childbirth and tuberculosis. If we look at average life remaining at age 65, the difference is only 5 years for men and 7 years for women (Table 9). People who reached adulthood in the pre-war years could expect to reach 75 (Yuzawa 1977a:176).

The increased life expectancy alone would not have changed the population structure drastically were it not for the rapid decline in the birth rate after 1955 (see Table 10). Thus the proportion of elderly in the population has risen at a very rapid rate, creating what is known in Japan as "the problem of the elderly". It is estimated that the shift in population structure from 8% to 18% in the 60 year or older group will occur in Japan in 40 years, a transition which took 177 years in France, 103 years in Sweden, and 54 years in West Germany (1978 Ministry of Health and Welfare figures, in Hasegawa 1981:197).

Compounding the "problem of the elderly" is the nuclearization of the family discussed earlier. Even if the proportion of elderly in the population remained stable, nuclearization would make them more visible and create problems of support. But, although the absolute number of nuclear families has risen dramatically, the proportion has increased more slowly (1960-60%, 1975-64%, 1982-68% [Yuzawa 1977a and Okayama 1984]).

In comparison with Western industrial societies (see Oikawa 1984), a large portion of the Japanese population over 60 lives within a three-generation family. The breakdown by family form for the 1982 population over 60 was: 11% of single person households; 19% of households with a married couple only; 10% in households composed of a married couple and their unmarried child(ren); 4% in households of a single parent and unmarried child(ren); 44% in three-generation households; and 12% in other types of households (Okayama 1984). Since the late 1960's, there has been a steady decline in the proportion of the elderly in three-generation households, and a rapid increase in the proportion in married couples only and in single person elderly households

TABLE 9
Changes in Japanese Average Life Expectancy

	1900-04	1926-30	1947	1960	1965	1970	1975	1980	1983
at birth: male	43.97	44.82	50.06	65.32	67.74	69.33	71.76	73.35	74.20
at birth: female	44.85	46.54	53.96	70.19	72.92	74.71	76.95	78.76	79.78
at age 65: male	10.14	9.64	10.16	11.62	11.88	12.47	13.76	14.50	15.19
at age 65: female	11.35	11.58	12.22	14.10	14.56	15.37	16.64	17.74	18.40

Data are from Ministry of Health and Welfare statistics: All dates through 1975 in Nihon Isnikai 1977:405; 1980 and 1983 figures in Ministry of Health and Welfare 1983 and UN Demographic Yearbook 1984.

TABLE 10
Changes in Population Structure
(unit: 10,000 people)

Year	A Total Population	B Population 65 and over	C Proportion of Elderly B/A x 100	D Elderly Dependency Ratio	E Youth Dependency Ratio	F Total Dependency Ratio
1880	3,629	243	6.7	10.3	43.2	53.5
1900	4,379	238	5.4	8.9	55.8	64.8
1920	5,539	292	5.3	9.0	62.6	71.6
1930	6,387	303	4.8	8.1	62.4	70.5
1935	6,866	319	4.6	7.9	63.1	71.1
1940						
1947	7,810	375	4.8	8.0	58.9	66.9
1950	8,320	411	4.9	8.3	59.3	67.5
1955	8,928	475	5.3	8.7	54.4	63.1
1960	9,342	535	5.7	8.9	46.8	55.7
1965	9,828	618	6.3	9.2	37.6	46.8
1970	10,467	739	7.1	10.2	34.7	44.9
1975	11,193	886	7.9	11.7	35.9	47.5
1980	11,756	1,044	8.9	13.2	35.8	49.0
1985	12,233	1,191	9.7	14.5	34.0	48.5
1990	12,628	1,391	11.0	16.2	30.8	47.0
1995	13,007	1,650	12.7	18.9	29.9	48.8
2000	13,368	1,906	14.4	21.7	30.8	52.5

$$D = \frac{B}{15\text{-}64 \text{ population}} \qquad E = \frac{\text{under 15 population}}{15\text{-}64 \text{ population}} \qquad F = D + E$$

In Yuzawa 1977b:174

(Figure 7). This change is more pronounced in urban than in rural areas (Okayama 1984; Ministry of Health and Welfare, 1983).

However, these statistics are not fully portraying the situation. Regional variation in nuclearization, for example, depends not only on the proportion of elderly in nuclear households, but also on the rate of elderly in the population (Shimizu 1984). Thus, a "conservative" rural village might have as high a proportion of elderly living alone or with a spouse as a Tokyo ward, because few young people remain in the village with whom they could live. On the other hand, parents and children who live next door in the Tokyo ward but have a high degree of mutual dependence would be counted as two separate nuclear families.

A final consideration to be addressed is to what extent ideology has changed. In a governmental survey of two groups, 1428 married men and women (31-50 years old - Group A and 1259 people 61-70 years of age - Group B), the majority of respondents felt that in general it is best for parents to live

with married children (Group A-68%, Group B-58%). There is even greater agreement that if one parent becomes physically weak, that the elder and younger
couples should live together (Group A-80%, Group B-84%). If one spouse dies,
the remaining parent is expected to live with a married child (Group A-83%,
Group B-84%). To the extent that behavior follows stated preference, many of
today's elderly nuclear families can be considered temporary arrangements.

FIGURE 7
Trends in Households with Persons Aged 65 and Over

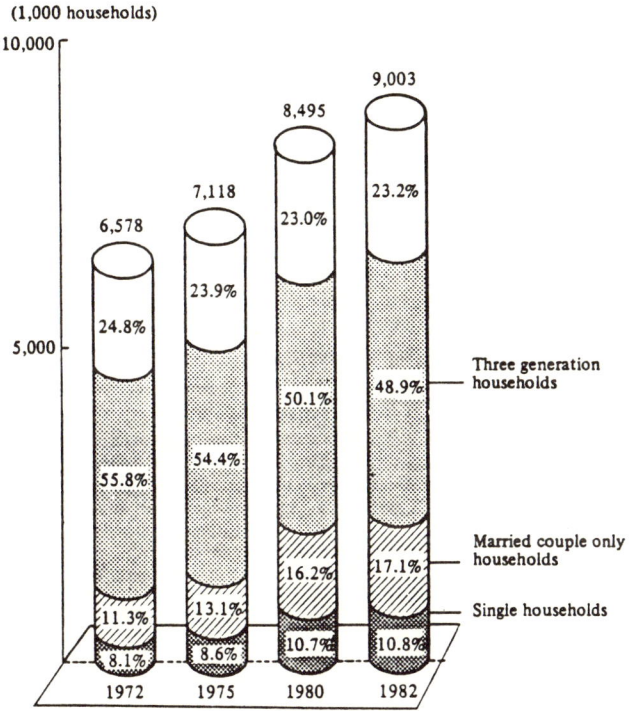

Source: "Basic Survey of Health and Welfare Administration",
Statistics & Information Department, MHW.
N.B. The white sections are for "households only with a
married couple and unmarried children", "households
only with a single parent and unmarried children" and
"other households".

In Ministry of Health and Welfare, 1984.

Harada has summarized the situation as follows:

(a) While nuclear family households have rapidly increased, extended Family households remain almost unchanged. The latter is said to have actually increased, when it is taken into consideration that the number of extended family households statistically comes out much smaller than the number of extended families, especially in recent years.

It is because economic development has caused an increase in such cases [as] staying away from home [due to] being employed in a far locality, sent out on business trips for more than 3 months, or transferred to local agencies for a few years. And as a result, many extended families were surveyed as two or more separated small households, though they were sharing household economy.

Thus nuclear family households increased to a remarkable degree with neither disorganization of extended families nor alternation of ideology. The increase was due to population of youngsters in marriageable age which was much greater in these 15 years than the population in the past. Accordingly, the increase of nuclear family households in Japan is not a real nucleating pattern which is commonly perceived in U.S.A. and other countries....

(b) The extended family households including old people 65 years old and over had a rise of 34% in 15 years. It is clarified that households with no old people, in other words, extended households including parents less than 65 years old have sharply decreased. The decrease concerns traditional family households which are, for example, a married couple with their parents, a couple with their children and parents, or a couple with children and a parent. In these families, there often happen such cases as the children who are supposed to live together with parents are employed in a different locality or transferred on business to another place. Those households thus separated are, most of them, to unite again with their parents' households, when they become much older. The increase of these households of temporary separation type also brought about the decrease of extended family households (English abstract, Harada 1978).

Yuzawa concludes that the major cause on the "problem of the elderly" lies not in demography but in politics and economics. The elderly do not want to be left behind in the trend toward an improved standard of living; yet the destruction of the _ie_ system has left them with a sense of insecurity regarding their ability to count on the support of relatives (Yuzawa 1977a:178-9).

The Three-Generation Family. A 1975 government survey found that 38% of the middle aged respondents were living with one or both parents. Co-residence was more common in non-urban than urban areas, among self-employed than employee families, among home owners than renters, among those with a high living standard than the poor, for eldest sons than other children, and for people providing parental support than those not providing such support. From the older generation's side, 75% (in the early 1980's about 70% of people

over 60 were living with a married or unmarried child and an additional 5%
were childless). Co-residence for the elderly was more common for women than
men, for single persons than married couples, among home owners than renters,
among those with a high living standard than the poor, and among those with
fewer years of schooling than the more highly educated. In the majority of
cases, parents live with a son and his spouse (63%), but 11% live with a
daughter and her husband, and 26% live with an unmarried child. Table 11 indicates the respondents' reported reasons for co-residence.

TABLE 11
Reason for Co-residence

Younger Generation		Older Generation	
It is a natural situation for a child to live with his parents	71%	It is a natural situation for a child to live with his parents	48%
Love for parents	12	To preserve the family and family business	19
Parents desired co-residence	4	Parent-child love	7
Economically advantageous	4	Child desired co-residence	4
Otherwise advantageous	4	Economic reasons	7
Parent's health is poor	2	Can get assistance from people around me	8
Other, unknown	3	Living alone is lonely	3
		Other, unknown	4

Data from Naikaku Sōri Daijin Kanbō Rōjin Taisaku Shitsu 1975:23, 53.

Yuzawa (1977a:194) summarizes the trends regarding co-residence: 1) the
focus of support is shifting from an economic problem to the problem of co- or
separate residence; 2) from unconditional continual co-residence to optional
co-residence based on conditions such as the parent's health; 3) from strong
co-residence bonds to "co-residence" in independent but neighboring quarters
to the extent possible; and 4) from co-residence of the young old to co-
residence of the middle or old old.

Those changes have resulted in great variations in membership, lifestyle, and extent of communal living among three generation families. The

Kansai Family Study Group has done the most extensive research on these families. They conducted a major survey in Osaka prefecture, urban and rural, in 1970 and 1971, and published the results in a multi-authored book entitled The Three Generation Family (Kamiko and Masuda 1976). They concluded that at the time of the study, the degree of communality in living arrangments (budget, household tasks, etc.) was very high (see Table 12). There were differences, however, between the urban and rural samples, leading several authors to utilize the concept of "modified stem family" (shusei chokkei kazoku). First used by Nasu (1967), a modified stem family refers to household that is stem in form, but contains relatively independent nuclear family units by which the younger couple retain greater autonomy than under the ie system. The modified stem family with its non-traditional power structure reflects a rational adaptation to modern circumstances. Kamiko and his colleagues believe that the modified stem family is a transitional form in the process of the nuclearization of the stem family. The modified stem family appears more often in urban than in rural areas, and more among upper and lower class than among middle class families.

Sodei Takako (1977) reviewed The Three Generation Family in the Japanese Sociological Review. Although she hails the book as a pioneering effort to study the internal structure of the stem family rather than merely its ideology, she criticizes the book on several accounts. The first set of criticisms involve methodology. She claims that 1) the authors' theoretical framework, research approach, and analytical scheme are not well spelled out; 2) the authors do not vigorously review existing literature as the basis for hypothesis formulation; 3) most of the analysis is limited to simple two-variable correlations (a problem recognized by Kamiko in the conclusion); 4) causal relations between the variables are not clear and the reader cannot distinguish between dependent and independent variables; 5) relations among the chapters are weak, to the extent that in one case, a family classified as middle class by the author of one chapter is considered upper class by another; 6) although women of both generations were surveyed, only data from one generation is utilized for each topic, thus limiting the conclusions that can be drawn on topics such as family discord.

Sodei's second set of criticisms point to areas in which further research is necessary. 1) The concept of the modified stem family needs to be clarified. Some authors evaluate it as modern and rational; others use it to indicate co-residing independent conjugal units. The fact that separate budgets are found more often in the upper and lower class than in middle class families points to the need for careful definition. 2) Life cycle stages need to be more clearly defined now that the increased life expectancy is leading to a longer time as a three-generation family. The authors use the criteria of relative financial burden and power relations to explain generational differences in responses, but they fail to consider other factors such as historical and ideological change. 3) There remains a need to develop a theoretical framework for the life of the three-generation family. Sodei points to the need to accumulate evidence over time, noting the tendency of Japanese researchers to concentrate on initial studies.

To me, the most impressive aspect of the book lies in its documentation of the tremendous diversity among three-generation families. There are those who want to co-reside and those who do not, differences in the roles and authority of the generations, those who eat together and those who share cooking but do not eat together, those in which a retiree contributes to the family income and those in which he or she relies on the younger generation for support. Tokuoka (in Kamiko and Masuda 1976) gives us a taste of this variation:

> Families with a single budget have strong instrumental, emotional, and moral bonds. ... When we look at the characteristics of the cases of totally separated budgets, we might wonder if we should even call them three generation families. But, for example, out of the 44 such cases, in only one of those could we consider it two separate families. Yet in this case, the families cook and eat together.

In a more recent study, Hasegawa (1984) surveyed and compared three-generation families of two types. In the first, a son and daughter-in-law lived with the parents, but the living quarters were actually divided into two households. She found that in such modified stem families, parents were economically independent, and that the two households rarely consulted each other concerning the grandchildren, had dinner or casual conversation together infrequently and rarely shared housework. In the other type of three-generation family Hasegawa studied, a daughter and son-in-law lived wth parents. In the majority of these cases, the two married couples behaved and thought of themselves as a single family unit, sharing budget, chores, dinner time, furniture, and child care concerns. She does not include a discussion of the traditional stem family's situation in which a married son and daughter-in-law share a residence with parents. Kamiko and his colleagues have attempted to find relationships in this variation, and to a large extent have succeeded, if not in creating a general theory, at least in formulating tentative conclusions that can be further tested.

TABLE 12
A Comparison of Survey Results on Communality in Three-Generation Families

			sharing a budget	lack of a private room for older generation	usually eat together
Osaka	-urban	1971	80%	21.2%	83.6%
	-rural	1971	98	27.1	99.0
National	-urban	1975	--	22	89
	-rural	1975	--	23	95
Tokyo	-urban	1971	91.8	19.6	93.7
	-urban	1977	88.5	12.3	92.2

Data calculated from:
Osaka, Kamiko, et al. 1976
National, Naikaku Sōri Daijin Kanbō Rōjin Taisaku Shitsu, 1975:24
Tokyo, Tokyo Elderly Welfare Basic Survey, in Naoi 1979:33.

Living Separately. There is a consensus among sociologists (Harada [1978] quoted above and Morgan and Hiroshima [1983] are the exceptions) that the trend is away from co-residence toward independent elderly households. Kamiko suggests four reasons for this trend: 1) a decrease in self-employment with urbanization, industrialization, and abandonment of farming; 2) improvement in public old age pensions which provide the economic basis for independence; 3) change in values regarding co-residence; and 4) higher standards of living. Reasons given by people actually not co-residing are shown in Table 13. Kamiko, et al. (n.d.b.) also found that external limitations were rarely mentioned as a reason for separate residence; their respondents more often chose to live separately for reasons of psychological comfort such as avoiding family conflict.

Among those living separately, over half live within one hour from at least one child (Naikaku...1975:29, 58; Naoi 1979:33), and according to a 1975 national government survey, of the middle aged respondents living separately from their parents, 23% visited them at least once a week, 30% visited once or twice a month, and 29% visited at least once a year (Naikaku... 1975:30). (The Detroit Area Study found that for urban Americans in 1956, frequency of contact with relatives was: at least once a week - 67%, once or twice a month - 20%. However, relatives in that survey also included collaterals [Blood, 1962]). The type of contact varies from ritual visits to discussions of problems, but it appears from several studies that elderly people living in independent households continue to count on their children for advice (Mitani

TABLE 13
Reasons for Separate Residence

Younger Generation		Older Generation	
Parent(s) living with another child	51%	--	
Because of marriage	19	Child (daughter only) is married	14%
Workplace too far from parents' home	10	Child's workplace too far away	42
Home too small	5	Home too small	5
Parents' desire separate residence	5	Child desires separate residence	12
Separate residence is more comfortable	3	Want to live more comfortably	14
Other, unknown	7	Other, unknown	9

From Naikaku Sōri Daijin Kanbō Rōjin Taisaku Shitsu 1975:24, 57.

1978), care when ill, financial assistance (Yamanaka 1976) when needed. It appears, however, that most independent elderly do not require assistance in their daily lives. Kamiko et al. (n.d.b:6) state that "practically all the old couples carry out major household tasks (cooking, laundry, shopping, bed making) by themselves." Only 25% in the middle-aged respondents living apart from their parents in the 1975 government survey reported providing assistance in daily activities to their parents. Nearly all who do not, stated that their parents manage on their own. Of the assistance that is provided, especially preparing meals, taking the parent when he or she needs to go out, and assistance with the toilet and bath were each chosen by about a one-fourth of the respondents (multiple answers possible) (Naikaku...1975:39-40).

Yamanaka (1981:234-5) suggests that the assistance, or the expectation of assistance if needed, strengthens the parent-adult child relationship when she discusses the relative estrangement of non-co-residing children when the parent(s) live(s) with another child. This relative estrangement may be due in part to remnants of the ie ideology, but also may be due to the physical distance involved, especially compared with co-residence. (See Uno 1976 regarding distance as a factor in grandparent-grandchild relations.)

As the Japanese family is transformed from an ie model to a nuclear model, two major problems are said to arise for the elderly. The first is economic support, the second, a sense of alienation. Under the ie system, retirement meant a shift in roles, but specific roles for the retired and the elderly did exist. Meiji law stipulated that adult children should financially assist elderly parents. The vast majority of Japanese today indicate a willingness to take in a widowed parent (see p. 64). People in the post-war era have also come to believe that society has a responsibility to develop pension and savings plans for support of the elderly (if not for their own parents, at least for the elderly in general). (See, for example, Naikaku... 1975:37). The proportion of people planning to depend on their children for support in their old age has dropped to less than half of the 1950 level (1950-59% vs. 1979-24%) (Ishihara 1982:127).

Actual support of parents has decreased as well in the post-war period, as Table 14 shows. In 1975, 40% of middle-aged people surveyed contributed to their parent(s)' living expenses, 62% of those providing the majority of their income. Of those not providing financial assistance, half said another child was doing so and another 31% said the parent(s) did not need the assistance. Of the elderly respondents, 45% received financial help, co-residing parents more than separately residing, women more than men, single more than married parents. Most received income from only one child. Of those not receiving financial assistance from a child, three-fourths stated they did not need it. Sixteen percent of the elderly respondents provided assistance to children 20 years and older, usually to one child. This assistance was most often all or part of their income, which I suspect applies largely to students and poorly paid new workers. However, 17% more provided a residence, 15% help with grand-children, and 16% assist with cooking or housework.

TABLE 14
Trends in Support of Elderly Living Expenses (people 65 and over)

	1957	1963	1973
Child support	76.6%	61.5%	55.6%
Income from work	17.6	16.6	12.7
Property and other income	1.2	7.6	3.9
Pensions (including social security)	2.5	9.1	12.5
Support from other than child	---	3.0	8.9
Welfare	2.1	2.2	4.2
Unknown	---	0.1	1.0

Data from Ministry of Health and Welfare Surveys, in Yamashita 1979:27.

The second problem arising from the trend toward separate residence concerns alienation of the elderly. However, evidence is inconsistent, and alienation seems to be more of an assumption than an empirical conclusion. Saito (1977:74) notes an increase in the number of old people with psychogeriatric disorders and Aoi (1978) points to the high suicide rate of the elderly, especially the old old. Hasegawa (1981:216-217) speculates that alienation results from disappointed expectations of co-residence, lack of communication between spouses after retirement due to separate interests and spheres of activity, a sense of uselessness, and loneliness, especially after the death of a spouse among separately residing elderly. Noda (1983) stresses the importance to the elderly of meaningful social participation, including group activities with the younger generation, for a sense of fulfillment.

In a small-scale study in northeastern Japan, Saito (1979:45-44) found that about half of his sample of persons 50 and older were oriented toward the happiness of their families. He also found that about three-quarters believed they had some useful contribution to make in their lives, although the proportion of women was greater than of men, and those in their 50's and 60's felt more useful than those over 70.

Evidence from other studies suggests that most elderly are relatively satisfied with their lives. Kawaai and Inoue (1980) compared women in the parental and post-parental stages of life and found the latter more content with their lives regardless of whether their focus was on work or family. Kamiko, et al. (n.d.b:6) conclude from their study of elderly in urban Osaka who live separately from their children that the morale of old people is high, noting that only 23% of men and 33% of women are anxious about their futures. Yamanaka's (1976) study provides evidence that separately residing elderly are not alienated from their neighbors. On the other hand, this satisfaction may not be evenly distributed among all Japanese. Matsushima (1983) points out that unmarried women, especially divorcees, have more concerns about their old age than married women in either the urban or rural sample. Concerns about receiving care if seriously ill are found more among those who are childless and among those whose health is already compromised, than among those who are healthy and have adult children.

Other researchers have analyzed life satisfaction by several variables. It does not seem well explained by socioeconomic factors alone (Hosoe 1980), although satisfaction with economic factors is important in newly retired men (Wada 1981:20). Occupational mobility experience, attitudes toward retirement (Wada 1981:20-21), and the quality of the husband-wife relationship (Hosoe 1980) may be significant. Saito (1977:172-173) hypothesized that old people living with their children would have a higher life satisfaction index (not defined) than those living separately. The hypothesis was borne out in two of the communities studied (Nada, Okinawa and a rapidly industrializing fishing village near Tokyo), but did not hold for the Tokyo sample. She suggests that urban residents may be experiencing greater satisfaction with separate residences, an observation that finds support in the work of Kamiko and his colleagues (see also Hasegawa 1984).

Kinship Relations

As I noted in the introductory section, the Japanese have utilized two different principles of kinship, the dōzoku and the shinrui (kindred). The major change in relations with relatives has been the breakdown of the dōzoku although its influence remains even among urban conjugal families.

The two principles coexisted in a variety of ways in traditional village society (Kitano and Masaoka 1975). Relations with a broader circle of relatives, including the families of one's wife and sister, were recognized, but kinship was most often thought of in terms of the dōzoku. The component units of extra-household kinship were the ie, rather than the individuals comprising it. Industrialization with its associated occupational geographical mobility undermined the dōzoku. Land reform and the new family law in the post-war period further weakened their influence (Yuzawa 1977b:50).

In the post-war family system, relations are based on the individual or on the conjugal couple. Koyama found a trend away from patrilineal predominance (associated with dōzoku) in a study of contacts with kin conducted in the 1960's. As indicated in Tables 15 and 16, families which were nuclear in form ("created families") generally reported less contact and less cooperative exchange than did stem families ("succeeded families"). Exceptions are dependence on relatives for finding a job and for child care. The frequency of contact with the wife's relatives (as opposed to the husband's) was greater in the urban sample than the rural (see Koyama 1966).

Sociologists have noted a shift in the relation between a woman and her mother-in-law. Masuda found increased tension in the mother-in-law/daughter-in-law relation in three-generation families and suggested that a reversal of the traditional power relation was taking place. With women's greater freedom of movement and of time, it is expected that the mother-married daughter tie will predominate as in the West (Yuzawa 1977b:51; Yamanaka 1981:231). Yamanaka warns, however, that we should not forget that there were traditional roles in regard to the birth and education of a daughter's children and obligations to visit in-laws. Masuda's study did not reveal major differences between the generations in what married women relied on their own parents to do (Yamanaka 1981:232).

TABLE 15

Percentages of Relatives (of All Relatives) with Whom Respondents Enter into Social Association of Various Types.

| | | usual associa-tion | Social Association | | | Rites de Passage | | | | Total |
			festivals	"Bon" festivals & year-end	new year's day	birth	Buddhist masses	marriage	funerals	
rural	**succeeded family**	Total	41·2	44·0	47·8	66·6	60·3	64·9	67·3	79·6	100·0% (N=2,816)
		relatives of husband	25·1	26·7	29·4	38·0	34·4	41·1	40·4	44·3	
		relatives of wife	16·1	17·3	18·4	28·6	25·9	23·8	26·9	35·3	
	created family	Total	42·5	43·9	51·8	59·5	54·3	56·3	58·4	68·8	100·0% (N=529)
		relatives of husband	24·6	24·8	30·2	32·1	29·7	31·2	31·2	36·1	
		relatives of wife	17·9	19·1	21·6	27·4	24·6	25·1	27·2	32·7	
urban	**succeeded family**	Total	38·2	23·1	44·7	66·3	48·2	59·8	62·5	70·1	100·0% (N=1,009)
		relatives of husband	16·7	11·3	21·8	30·4	22·5	31·9	32·2	34·4	
		relatives of wife	21·5	11·8	22·9	35·9	25·7	27·9	30·3	35·7	
	created family	Total	29·3	18·2	37·4	61·5	37·5	49·3	54·3	67·1	100·0% (N=2,516)
		relatives of husband	14·3	9·2	19·1	31·4	19·3	26·2	28·8	35·3	
		relatives of wife	15·0	9·0	18·3	30·1	18·2	23·1	25·5	31·8	

From Koyama 1966:112

TABLE 16

Percentages of Relatives (of All Relatives) with Whom Respondents Co-operate for Various Items of Help.

		consult on all matters	help for busy work	help for marriage	help for finding jobs	help for the care of children	help for the care of sick persons	lending or borrowing of money	help at time of calamity	Total
rural	**succeeded family**	Total	33·1	15·6	19·4	10·2	3·8	7·7	9·1	25·5	100·0% (N=2,816)
		relatives of husband	20·3	9·2	11·5	5·7	2·1	4·4	5·8	14·4	
		relatives of wife	12·8	6·4	7·9	4·6	1·7	3·3	3·3	11·1	
	created family	Total	31·4	13·8	16·3	8·9	4·1	8·7	11·1	28·5	100·0% (N=529)
		relatives of husband	17·6	7·6	8·7	5·3	1·3	5·5	6·2	17·0	
		relatives of wife	13·8	6·2	7·6	3·6	2·8	3·2	4·9	11·5	
urban	**succeeded family**	Total	26·4	12·0	13·8	11·1	7·1	8·6	9·0	22·6	100·0% (N=1,009)
		relatives of husband	12·9	5·5	6·2	4·7	3·1	3·6	4·2	11·9	
		relatives of wife	13·5	6·5	7·6	6·4	4·0	5·0	4·8	10·7	
	created family	Total	23·3	10·7	13·3	8·3	4·7	9·2	9·1	23·3	100·0% (N=2,516)
		relatives of husband	12·1	4·2	6·7	4·6	1·7	4·2	5·3	12·9	
		relatives of wife	11·2	6·5	6·6	3·7	3·0	5·0	3·8	10·4	

From Koyama 1966:113

Another aspect of the traditional legacy can be seen in sibling relations. The weakness of the sibling tie is expressed in a saying which might
be loosely translated as, "Siblings are the closest strangers" (Yamanaka
1981:228). Masaoka explains that in the ie system, the structuring of authority based on lineality, age, and birth order would tend to destroy the development of close sibling relations particularly between siblings of the same
sex. A man was likely to have a warmer relationship with his wife's brothers
than with his own (Masaoka 1975:25). Actual surveys of frequency of contact
among relatives differentiate between contacts with parents and contacts with
siblings, but results do not appear to be consistent. Meguro suggests the
nature of parent-child ties and sibling ties differs, with the later more
likely to be used instrumentally (Meguro 1974b). Birth order, number of siblings, and wife's versus husband's side may or may not be significant variables in these contact surveys. Educational level and social class do not
seem to be important factors. (Koyama 1966, Morioka et al. 1968, Uhashi and
Shimizu 1972, Meguro 1974a, Iwagami 1976, Sashida 1981). Differentiating
every-day and ritual contacts seems to be important due to the obligatory
nature of participation in the ie system. The type of contact may also help
to clarify the situation. Iwagami (1976:84) found that telephoning was common
between a woman and her own sisters and that letter writing to older brothers
was a frequent means of contact.

The studies reporting frequency of contact, taken together, do not provide a clear cut picture of ties among collaterals. However, responses to a
cross-national opinion poll question are striking. The survey asked young
respondents the hypothetical question: "Your grandmother, whose husband recently died, expresses a desire to live with someone. What would you do if
you were your parents (the woman's child)? Your close aunt (the woman's
niece)? A close friend?" The proportion of respondents who said they would
take them in is shown in Table 17. The great majority of both Japanese and

TABLE 17
Responses to Whether People Would Take in Grandmother

	if parent	if aunt	if close friend
Japan	86%	20%	8%
United States	84%	69%	52%

Source: Tokyo Gerontology Research Center
In Yamanaka 1981:227-228 and in Sussman & Romeis 1981, 1982.

American respondents indicate a willingness to take in a parent, but a much smaller proportion of Japanese respondents would take in an aunt or a friend than the American group.

The scholar who has made the greatest attempt to systematize the information on kinship is Masaoka Kanji. He argues that studies which limit their consideration to distinctions between blood and marriage ties, geneological distance, patrilineal and matrilineal ties, and so on fail to look at the whole picture. Such approaches can never explain processes such as the enlargement or shrinkage of the kin group. Masaoka has developed a model based on a distinction between immediate (mediating) relatives, mediated relatives (the tie being through another relative, and over which ego's control is minimal), and distant relatives (kin whom ego meets on ritual occasions such as funerals but to whom no links are traced). Table 18 represents his formulation of kinship differences between the ie and the modern family. He notes that ie-based kinship was based on membership (defined patrilineally) in the corporate group rather than on blood ties; even the dead continued to be considered kin. Kin ties and associated rights and obligations came with ie membership, and kin generally shared common social, cultural, and geographical bases. On the other hand, in the modern conjugal family, major distinctions are between ties of blood and marriage and between living and dead. Kinship ties extend both patrilineally and matrilineally and cover a wider social and geographical sphere. Ties are based on individual preference and on emotion and ethical considerations which may not be shared across the kin network. Masaoka believes these differences are best explained by a dynamic model such as his based on mediation (Masaoka 1975:10-26).

Meguro has also moved away from a functionalist approach to kinship by using social network analysis and exchange theory (Meguro 1974b, in English see Meguro 1974a). In a later report, she combined this with the family cycle and historical approaches on a limited scale by reinterviewing five of the families of her 1970 study five years later. She found that changes in family cycle and in society which have occurred during that time are reflected in changes in the family's social network, resulting in the shifting balance of needs and resources. Masaoka, Meguro and others are arguing for a move away from cross-sectional data to more theoretical and intensive studies of kin relations.

TABLE 18 Systematization of Kinship Relations ——
A Comparison of the Ie and the Modern Family

	Basis of Systematization of Kinship Relations	Kinship in the Ie System	Kinship in the Modern Family
Primary Elements		deep, broad	shallow, narrow
	1. genealogical position and distance		
	2. distinction between ties of blood and ties of marriage	weak	yes
	3. distinction between generations	yes	yes
	4. distinction between sexes	yes	no
	5. distinction between patrilineal and matrilineal	yes (patrilineal)	weak (matrilineal)
	6. distinction between lineal and collateral	yes	yes
	7. distinction by age and birth order	yes	no
	8. distinction between living and dead	weak	yes
	9. functional replacement	possible	impossible
Secondary Elements	1. ideology of kinship relations	systemic, imperative	ethical
	2. extent of authority and obligations	comprehensive	partial
	3. permissible social distance	small	large
	4. permissible geographical distance	small	large
	5. individual selectivity	no	yes
	6. differences in kin culture within kin group	similar	different

Nasaoka 1975:12

Opinions about the Family

Opinion surveys on the family by both government agencies and sociologists have been numerous. I will not attempt a comprehensive review of the material, but rely mainly on Yuzawa's (1977b) discussion of national trends.

Opinions about the ie have changed greatly in the post-war period. A Mainichi Newspaper Company survey in 1947 found that 58% of respondents agreed that the ie system should be abolished. In 1956 the majority of people surveyed by the Prime Minister's Office supported traditional family relations, but from the 1960 Constitution Survey, supporters of the new family system became the majority. By 1966, such support reached two-thirds. In the 1950's, advocates of the new family system were mostly young, but by the 1960's, middle-aged and older people were also agreeing with the "new" ways (Yuzawa 1977b:54).

One aspect of the ie system remains supported by public opinion, that of co-residence. Although wording and choice differences of questions in various surveys make comparison difficult, at least half of survey respondents think co-residence is the best situation. Yuzawa concludes that both men and women prefer co-residence to separate residence (as a matter of general opinion), particularly older people. However, recently a sense of conditionality has grown stronger (Yuzawa 1977a:182). It should be noted, however, that in the earlier survey, Yuzawa considered from 1966, conditional co-residence was not among the questionnaire choices. If any form of co-residence (including a modified stem family type) is included, opinions favoring co-residence may have even increased.

Although family may be differently defined, it has remained important to individual Japanese. In the National Character Survey conducted every 5 years by the Statistical Research Center, respondents are asked what is most important to them. The largest number of people selected "family, children" in 1953, 1958, and 1973, competing for first place over the 20 years with the response "life, health". Evidence from other surveys as well leads Yuzawa (1977b:53-54) to conclude that "family centrism" remains strong. Nearly half of the respondents in a 1980 survey, when asked their major life goal, chose "a peaceful, harmonious family life" (Sōrifu Hōkokushitsu 1981:31-2).

Moreover, Yuzawa claims that the Japanese family today is maintained by traditional or conservative values. A 1972 survey asked people their purpose in life. Among women, the most common response was their children (not their spouse); among men, family was chosen second most often after work. Women continue to gain satisfaction from child-rearing and home management, and 80% are satisfied with their relationships with husbands. Men and women alike oppose free sex and easy divorce, opinions which are seen to be "anti-familial" (Yuzawa 1977b:55).

FAMILY CYCLE AND LIFE COURSE IN JAPAN

The Family Cycle Framework

The family cycle approach has become popular in Japanese family sociology, particularly among the Tokyo-based researchers, due to the influence of
Morioka Kiyomi. Using ideas from American rural sociology and modifying concepts or models from the work of Koyama and Suzuki, Morioka has developed a
framework that has prepared fertile ground for life course concepts such as
transition.

Morioka notes several uses of family cycle in the Japanese literature.
1) Family cycle may be used to explain and predict variation in household
composition. Koyama's (1959) study follows this approach. 2) Stage of family
cycle may be used as an independent variable, as Suzuki did in the earliest
Japanese work on family cycle as it related to economic activities. 3)
Morioka's own approach has been to consider each stage of the life cycle as a
role complex and to trace changes in it across the stages. He refers to this
as being within the developmental approach (Morioka 1967b:596; 1973:337).
Although his earlier methodology involved cross-sectional analysis, he later
utilized longitudinal and cohort analyses (Morioka 1973).

Morioka's model is a three stage cycle of the stem family. Stage I begins with the marriage of the heir and lasts until the death of his father;
Stage II lasts from the end of Stage I until the death of his mother; Stage
III is a nuclear family from the death of the mother until the marriage of his
eldest son (heir). Portions of Morioka's Family Cycle Theory (1973), his
major work on family cycle, are available in English (Morioka 1967b, 1981) and
Ishihara (1981b) has translated some relevant tables. While he is aiming at
the third approach to life cycle (stage = role complex), much of the 1973 book
takes the second approach in which stage of family cycle is an independent
variable in investigating changes in educational expenses, living expenses,
housing, and sleeping arrangements in the family.

Other researchers have followed this approach. In The Life Cycle of the
Modern Family (Morioka 1977), Okada examines changes in family budgets,
Shimanouchi in health management, and Meguro (Nojiri) in social networks,
according to changes in family cycle stage (e.g., the oldest child starting
school, or the youngest graduating). Sugaya (1980) has related cycle stage to

the development of relationships among wives in a new residential area, showing that the quality of a relationship changes with the family stage of an individual and depending on whether the other person is at the same or a different stage. Sugioka (1978) asks similar questions about the relation between family cycle stage and agricultural cooperatives in rural families. Takahashi (1980) discusses the questions of housing, co-residence, and support for the elderly in terms of their changing needs at different stages of being old (young old vs. old old). By relating family cycle to agricultural and non-agricultural labor, Matsumura (1979) challenges the idea that an increase in side work (non-agricultural) necessarily leads to the breakdown of the stem family and the abandonment of agriculture.

Other studies have emphasized the developmental aspect of the family cycle. Although a few cover several stages, as in Satake's (1977) study of marital conflict, most focus on a transitional period, Mochizuki (1977) on the period preceding marriage, Okamura (1977) on retirement, Kakizaki (1977) and Ishihara (1977) on succession. Yuzawa (1972) notes that stressful periods for families include yōshi adoption, remarriage, marital conflict, death, and the experience of natural disasters, although he does not refer to a specific family cycle model. Ishihara (n.d.b.) studied stress in relation to life course transitions, emphasizing migration as a major transition. He found that recent migrants scored lower than rural or urban long-time residents on indices of satisfaction with community and family life and had worse mental health conditions. Urban residents generally had higher amounts of social stress than rural residents.

The volume edited by Morioka (1977) received mixed reviews. Yokoyama's criticisms seem to me to be valid and important. He points out that Morioka as well as several of the book's contributors recognize that the family cycle approach does not deal adequately with the diversity of their samples. And yet, they continue to attempt to define a standard family cycle. He further argues that using the ie model for farm families is no longer appropriate given the attitudinal and behavioral changes of the post-war period (Yokoyama 1979:76). Chūbachi (1976), who coordinated a series of studies on household expenses over the family cycle, attempted to break the middle and older years into stages in considering the relation of family form to household budget, nutrition and health. But he too fails to overcome the problem of the tremendous variation in life goals and longer personal histories of older adults (Meguro 1978).

Life Course Research on Japan

As a conscious sociological model, the life course is relatively new to Japan. The family cycle approach, concerned with timing and transitions, has been used widely, however. It has treated the family as a group of related individuals rather than as a corporate institution. Thus, Ishihara (1981a) has easily been able to incorporate the life course approach into his work on succession.

Two types of studies relate directly to the life course perspective. The first deals with aggregate data. The Citizen's Life Center (Kokumin Seikatsu Sentā 1976) has collected data on the family histories, residential, histories, and work careers of urban families, and has analyzed it by marriage cohort. Sodei (1978) notes, however, that the sample is small and that differences between cohorts are not always statistically significant. Because the three types of histories are analyzed separately, the writers neglect to discuss the interrelationships among the family, residential, and work histories. A study by the Labor Science Research Institute (Fujimoto 1978) considers changes in the life cycles of laborers, employed women, and farmers as influenced by economic growth, inflation, and recession; but is limited to cross-sectional analysis of survey responses.

A major study on the life course was begun in 1982 by the Family and Life Course Study Group, headed by Morioka Kiyomi. The research focused on four cohorts of men between the ages of 45 and 64, and it includes a large-scale survey of occupational and other careers, plus intensive interviews of a sub-sample of 31 individuals and their wives. Furthermore, the research design was three generational, so that questionnaires were also distributed to the parents and children of the original sample. Interviewees were asked to identify "turning points" and "events difficult to solve" and the timing of these transitions. Questions included information on support networks and on timing in occupational and family careers. In their 1985 English language volume, Family and Life Course of Middle Aged Men (Morioka 1985), the researchers use survey and life history material to discuss the effects of experiencing WWII and the high economic growth years of the 1960's. They investigate intergenerational continuities and changes, individual success and the life course, co-residence, and intergenerational solidarity. Each author analyzes specific portions of the data, but the presentations are not integrated and English-language terminology varies from one chapter to another.

The book is important, however, not only for presenting new data, but for pointing out problems and benefits in utilizing the life course approach cross-culturally. By explicitly employing methodologies comparable to those of American research projects, the authors can state comparative conclusions such as that the transition to adulthood takes place over a longer time-span in Japan (Mochizuki et al. 1985 and Hogan 1981). Normative intergenerational solidarity has decreased in both U.S. and Japan (Morioka, et al. 1985 and Bengtson et al. 1976). In general, statistical analyses can produce such comparisons. Yet problems appear in the translation of terms and in the interpretation of concepts. An entire chapter (Chapter 3) is devoted to exploring the concept of a turning point as understood by respondents. The authors found that when asked to name a single turning point in their lives, educated respondents answered the question more readily than those with less schooling. Masaoka and his colleagues found, moreover, that for people in the Shizuoka sample who had experienced a turning point that it was less a "point" than a process of altering a lifepath: a "course correction." It began with a piling up of significant events, took place over a period of years, and required resolution. "We can infer that the more distinct one's resolution and destination in a certain situation, the stronger one's consciousness of a turning point in later life." (Masaoka 1985:104). It appears that a sense of having experienced a turning point itself depends on one's social development during and after a series of events. Is "turning point" as these authors use it, a kind of subjectively defined "transition"?

Another area of difficulty lies in the Japanese perception that the underlying basis of the life course approach is individualism. This issue is dealt with indirectly in this volume by Ishihara and colleagues (1985) who introduce the concept of "family career", and by Hamaguchi (1985) who contrasts "individual" and "contextual" social careers. (See also Hamaguchi 1979.)

The second approach within the life course perspective views life history as social process, or what Plath terms "social chronology". Tsurumi's work relates adult socialization to historical events. Using personal documents and intensive interviews, she investigated the relation between the individual and social change as a result of Japan's defeat in World War II and through participation in the student movement of 1960 (Tsurumi 1970). Another researcher has turned to life history as a method of evaluating the relationship of the individual to society. Nakano (1982) believes that, through the personal relationship established in this approach, stereotypes can be avoided and sociology reinfused with a human image of social life. In his book, Life History by Aural Personal Document: A Women's Love and Hatred Reflecting Modern Japan (1977), he analyzes the autobiography of an 85-year-old woman who experienced life as a Manchurian colonist, went to Korea during a second marriage, and has witnessed the rapid industrialization and pollution of the Mizushima (Kurashiki) area in recent years. Through her life story, events overlooked by political historians take on meaning and historical trends acquire new interpretations. Nakano's goal is to create a new typology of social and individual change, but he believes this can only come from sociological comparison of accumulated case histories. (See review by Tsurumi 1982.)

Lebra (1984) has accomplished this for a sample of Japanese women in her book, Japanese Women: Constraint and Fulfillment (1984). Drawing upon open-ended interviews with individuals, group interviews, and participant observation, she identifies roles and turning points in family and occupational careers. She explores issues of intergenerational continuity and the adaptability of Japanese women in their response to the male-dominated social order. Individuals respond differently to changing social circumstances, yet Lebra identifies patterns of response, strategies developed by her informants to prepare for incompletely defined future situations (see also Lebra 1979 and 1981).

Plath has done the most to utilize the life course perspective as a coherent framework for viewing Japanese society. Maturing proceeds over the life course in a social context of "long engagements" with others, as one struggles against the historical circumstances in which he or she experiences life. The process itself depends on local idioms, however (Plath 1980). Rohlen (1976) writes that cultural notions of adulthood in Japan differ from those in the West, that the definition of adulthood (if not the daily reality) centers on personal growth rather than the sense of decay that has permeated post-industrial attitudes toward aging. Hamaguchi (1985) points out that "career" refers not only to an individual's unique movement through a series of roles, but that "we must recognize that one's unique 'career' is in fact produced in the network of one's human relations." He believes that Japanese are more likely to think of life courses as embedded in social relations, that "career" means, to the Japanese, a "lifelong history of the human nexus." Plath (1982) has suggested that in contrast to Americans, Japanese might also have a longer time perspective on human development and on human relationships.

THE FUTURE: THE JAPANESE FAMILY
AND THE LIFE COURSE APPROACH

I have reviewed literature dealing with changes in the Japanese family
over the past several hundred years and analyzed it in relation to the life
course approach in history and sociology. Before concluding, I want to offer
my own speculations about the future. How is the Japanese family changing?
What may happen next in life course research in Japan?

Social Change and the Japanese Family

Studies of family change overwhelmingly point to the adaptabilty and re-
sponsiveness of Japanese families to wider social and economic circumstances.
Throughout Japanese history, we see not only diachronic shifts in such things
as family form, inheritance practices, and family planning, but also synchronic variation according to local and household circumstances.

The origins of the ie as a system remain a subject of debate and discussion (for example, see Journal of Japanese Studies 10[4] and 11[1], 1985).
The formulation of the ie model as a basis for family law and citizen behavior
is a well documented event of the late 19th century. To what extent individual households have consciously or unconsciously acted in accordance with ie
principles is an empirical question which much of the work I have discussed
has attempted to answer.

Researchers have also documented the decline in the influence of the ie
model over the 20th century in response to industrialization and to occupation-
induced legal reform. In studying this transition, we need to keep in mind
that in the long span of Japanese history, there is no single "traditional"
family type. Likewise, what some would view as remnants of "the traditional
family" could be better seen as the product of flexible adjustment of lifestyles to daily reality. The persistence of multigeneration families as well
as the increase in single-person households suggests to me not cultural lag,
but an expanded cultural repertoire from which individuals draw in making
decisions about their lives. Change has been neither unidirectional nor continual. As Goode predicted, industrialization has created pressures for
change in the family, but such change has been modified by political concerns,
by problems of a postindustrial society, and by efforts of individual families.

That family forms and meanings in Japan will converge with those in Western postindustrial societies is not a foregone conclusion. Statistical trends may not accurately reflect opinions or predict future behavior. The existence of a higher proportion of two-generation households in 1980 than in 1920 masks the continuing emphasis on lineality in Japanese families. Parent-child ties are assumed in Japan to predominate over those between husband and wife or among siblings. Many Japanese, both researchers and the public, continue to find it difficult or unrealistic to view the family as a mere collection of individuals. Morioka (1984b) argues that the 20th century has shown a trend towards privatization of the family, reflecting a diminution of dōzoku, extended kin, and neighborhood ties. However, the unit of "privacy" in Japan is not the individual, but the nuclear family, especially the conjugal couple. One might conclude that if this trend continues, it will lead to increased emphasis on the individual, but such a conclusion may be hasty. As long as a high degree of gender role complementarity continues, the family may remain a highly integrated and interdependent unit.

What of the persistence of "tradition"? Morgan and Hirosima (1983) convincingly argue that the three-generation family in contemporary Japan is an adaptive strategy by which kin attempt to handle several specific problems: low incomes in early occupational careers of men, old age security and support, the high cost of land, low retirement age, and the desirability of a wife's supplementary income. These functions of the three-generation family can and do coexist with expectations about role relations (such as between husband and wife, or between mother-in-law and daughter-in-law) which are not part of the ie model. Likewise, Morioka (1984a) points out that ancestor worship in contemporary Japan is not some functionless holdover, it has taken on new meanings which reflect today's society. Hardacre (1984) documents that at least one of the "new religions", Reiyūkai, consciously creates and utilizes "tradition" to achieve its spiritual and practical goals.

In their discussion of the co-residence of married children with parents, Kamiko and Noguchi (1985) suggest that there are conflicting trends not only in society, but within each individual as well. I do not think that they are implying that Japanese are filled with guilt and psychological conflict over whether to be "traditional" or "modern". Rather, as contemporary Japanese, they recognize a range of options, each with advantages and disadvantages to be weighed in reaching a decision about what is best for the family as a whole, and the individuals who comprise it.

Japanese Family Studies and the Life Course Approach

What then about the "fit" of the life course approach to studies of family change in Japan. To some extent this is a matter of "cultural translation" that involves social issues. Methodological concerns present fewer translation problems than do analytic concepts, but conceptual issues offer an opportunity for "re-translations" which may refine and revise the whole life course perspective.

The methods used by the scholars whose work I have reviewed are, in general, appropriate to life course-oriented studies. The work of Hayami and others using pre-modern population registers and documents seems particularly well-suited to life course analysis despite numerous difficulties with the historical sources. Hayami (1973), for example, demonstrates an ability to deal with variation in the timing of some life course events based on the reconstruction of individual life histories.

Sociological studies of the modern family are based primarily on survey data. Few studies have produced longitudinal data. The idea of analysis by marriage cohort seems to be relatively new. Recently, some sociologists have turned to case studies of life histories, but as Ishihara (1981b:10) points out, no one has bridged the gap between the macro and the micro approaches. The recent introduction of life course methods into mainstream Japanese family sociology offers such an opportunity.

Japanese researchers also deal with aggregate data that requires taking into account the diversity within a generation. They do so by analyzing data by class, residence (especially rural-urban), education, and occupation. Variables that are common in American studies (such as ethnicity or religion) do not appear in the materials that I have reviewed. I suspect this has to do with an image of Japanese cultural homogeneity that emphasizes conformity rather than variation. I return to this point below.

Several conceptual issues illustrate some of the difficulties in "translating" a set of ideas. American life course researchers have raised problems of definition of the terms "cohort" and "generation" (see Kertzer 1983). In the Japanese work, note the term "cohort" is used directly without translation in numerous studies as a means of dealing with aggregate data, in other words, at an analytical rather than empirical level. Generation refers primarily to biological relationships of ascendants and descendants. However there exists

an ill-defined sense of social generation regarding the experience of historical events (e.g., the Meiji Restoration, World War II) or periods (e.g., pre-
war education, rapid post-war economic growth). Thus, in the case of "cohort," the English term is used for precise meaning: in the case of "generation," there is an exact translation of the English word, but it also carries
the ambiguities which make it problematic in American studies.

Another type of problem appears with the concept of "developmental
stake." Developed by Bengtson and his colleagues (see Bengston 1976), this
term refers to the differential investments that a parent and an adult child
make in their relationship, which colors their perceptions of that relationship. The elder generation, for example, maximizes the affective aspects of
the relationship and minimizes differences in values or in exchanges of services, in an effort to emphasize intergenerational continuity and their own
worth. Although Japanese research results are consistent with Bengtson's
ideas, "developmental stake" has not been used as a concept. One reason for
this may be the existence of a folk concept, ongaeshi (see Benedict 1946:102
"debtor to the ages"), which is similar and unquestionably "natural" to members of Japanese society. Research shows that both power (e.g., inheritance,
succession, old age dependency) and emotional ties can form the basis of intergenerational solidarity. There may have been a movement from the former to
the latter, or at least a shift in the power relations between the generations. There has certainly been a change in solidarity of the broader circle
of relatives. With the breakdown of the dōzoku, the main household lost its
power over branch households. This implies a decrease in kin brokerage. However, instrumental kin ties continue to be important, particularly at critical
transitions such as marriage, obtaining employment, and death.

In "translating" the life course approach, we also find examples of differences in nuance due to cultural context. For example, the English "time"
and the Japanese "jikan" seem to be equivalent and should not present problems
in translation. I have heard the English "timing" (taimingu) freely used in
Japanese conversation in the context of "good timing" or "poor timing." Yet
in their study of the lives of middle aged men, the Japanese family sociologists (who themselves understand the way concepts of timing and transition are
used in American work) had to struggle to phrase questions in ways that would
be meaningful for their subjects. In doing so and in analyzing their results,
these scholars have had to modify definitions of such concepts as transition
and turning point. "Timing" as an approach remains difficult to deal with in

Japan. Perhaps this is <u>because</u> normative timetables are so strong in Japan. There may be a tendency to emphasize conformity to such a timetable and to ignore or even hide deviation as a source of embarrassment. This suggests that the failure of an individual to match the timetable is both a reflection on, and negatively affects, other family members, which itself is a fascinating area of research.

Finally, Japanese sociologists are asking whether the individualistic premise which they perceive in the life course perspective is a realistic way to approach the study of their society. Many of the scholars whose work I have reviewed here seem open to the approach and accept its utility, and yet, I still sense a difference. To many Japanese researchers, the family remains a <u>unit</u> even when life course concepts are utilized (e.g., Ishihara personal communication; Anonymous 1981). This may not be a cultural difference but a legacy of other academic approaches. The continued strong role differentiation within the Japanese family may also be a factor, making it difficult, for example, to conceptualize fatherhood apart from its place in the functional division of labor between husband and wife. I do <u>not</u> believe the difficulty can be directly attributed to unconscious assumptions the researchers themselves hold about the "traditional" family. But there may be differences in the questions being asked due to differences in the nature of what is being studied.

This issue is not a new one for Japanese scholars, but has roots in the sociological debates between Aruga and Toda, and more recently, between Yamamuro and Morioka, or the controversy surrounding <u>Rethinking the Nuclear Family</u>. If Japanese life course researchers must now make a distinction between individual as family member and family as a cluster of individuals, it seems to me that their work can also challenge unquestioned assumptions of Western life course work, and emphasize the importance of those whom Plath (1980) calls "consociates," people whose life courses are intimately intertwined with one's own.

The life course approach is new to Japanese researchers. I have shown that there is a willingness and the academic precedent to incorporate this perspective, as Hayami and Ishihara and their colleagues are already doing. Problems inherent in cross-cultural studies such as translation of concepts and differences in underlying assumptions will remain to be worked out. This process will not only provide us with cross-cultural data, but also with better theory for an understanding of the <u>human</u> life course.

BIBLIOGRAPHY

Aldous, Joan and Kamiko Takeji. 1972. A cross-national study of the effects of father-absence: Japan and the United States. In Cross-national family research. Marvin B. Sussman and Betty E. Cogswell, eds. Leiden: E.J. Brill.

Anonymous. 1981. A brief scheme of a research proposed by the Japanese team. U.S.-Japan comparisons on the family and the life course. Unpublished ms.

Aoi, Kazuo. 1978. The meaning of life for Japanese elderly. Paper presented at the 11th International Congress of Gerontology, August 24, Tokyo.

Aoi, Kazuo and Shōji Kōkichi. 1980. Kazoku to cniiki no shakaigaku (The sociology of the family and community). Tokyo: University of Tokyo Press.

Aoi, Kazuo and Yuzawa Yasuhiko. 1981. Family relations and the elderly of Japan. One proposal on U.S.-Japan comparative study. Unpublished ms.

Aoi, Kazuo, et al. 1970. Comparative study of home discipline: Rural-urban, sex and age differences. In Families in east and west. Reuben Hill and René Konig, eds. The Hague: Mouton.

Aoi, Kazuo, et al. 1981. Teinen taishoku go no shokugyōidō to seikatsu tekiō (Occupational mobility and adaption after mandatory retirement). Teinensei Mondai Kenkyukai.

Aoi, Kazuo, et al. 1985. Success and turning points in the life course. In Family and life course of middle-aged men. Morioka Kiyomi, ed. Tokyo: Family and Life Course Study Group.

Arichi, Tōru. 1976. Kindai Nihon ni okeru minshū no kazokukan (Attitudes of common people toward the family in the early Meiji period). In Kazoku: Seisaku to hō 7, Kindai Nihon no kazokukan. Fukishima Masao, ed. Tokyo: University of Tokyo Press.

Arichi, Tōru. 1981. Genkin no sōzoku no kinō no henka to sono kangaekata no saikentō (Functional change in present day succession and the reinvestigation of its way of thinking). Kazoku Shi Kenkyu 3:93-115.

Aruga, Kizaemon. 1954. The family in Japan. Marriage and Family Living 16:362-368.

Aruga, Kizaemon. 1956. Introduction to the family system in Japan, China, and Korea. Transactions of the 3rd World Congress of Sociology 4:199-207.

Atoh, Makoto Nohara. 1981. On the recent fertility decline in Japan. Shakaigaku Hyōron (Japanese Sociological Review) 31(4):91-97.

Bachnik, Jane. 1983. Recruitment strategies for household succession: Rethinking Japanese household organization. Man 18:160-182.

Befu, Harumi. 1962. Corporate emphasis and patterns of descent in the Japanese family. In Japanese culture: Its development and characteristics. Robert J. Smith and Richard K. Beardsley, eds. Chicago: Aldine Publishing Co.

Befu, Harumi. 1963. Patrilineal descent and personal kindred. American Anthropologist 65:1328-1341.

Befu, Harumi. 1968. Ecology, residence, and authority: The corporate household in central Japan. Ethnology 7:25-42.

Benedict, Ruth. 1946. The chrysanthemum and the sword. Cleveland, Ohio: The World Publishing Co.

Bengtson, Vern L. and Joseph A. Kuypers. 1971. Generational difference and the developmental state. Aging and Human Development 2:249-260.

Bengtson, Vern L. and Neal E. Cutler. 1976. Generations and intergenerational relations. In The handbook of aging and the social sciences. R. Binstock and E. Shanas, eds. New York: Van Nostrand Reinhold.

Bengtson, Vern L., et al. 1976. The "generation gap" and aging family members: Toward a conceptual model. In Time, roles, and self in old age. Jaber F. Gubrium, ed. Human Sciences Press.

Bernstein, Gail Lee. 1983. Haruko's world: A Japanese farm woman and her community. Stanford: Stanford University Press.

Blood, Robert O. 1962. Marriage. New York: Free Press.

Blood, Robert O., Jr. 1967. Love marriage and arranged marriage. New York: Free Press.

Brown, Keith. 1966. Dōzoku and the ideology of descent in rural Japan. American Anthropologist 68:1129-1151.

Brown, Keith. 1979. Shinjo: Chronicle of a Japanese village. University Center International.

Caudill, William and David Plath. 1966. Who sleeps by whom? Parent-child involvement in urban Japanese families. Psychiatry 29:344-366.

Caudill, William and Helen Weinstein. 1969. Maternal care and infant behavior in Japan and America. Psychiatry 32:12-43.

Chūbachi, Masayoshi, ed. 1976. Kōreika shakai no kazoku shūki (Family cycle in an aging society) Shiseidō.

Chūbachi, Masayoshi, ed. 1978. Family life cycle and intergenerational support: Survey on the Life of middle and old aged household, pt. 2. Tokyo: Shiseidō.

Coleman, Samuel. 1983. Family planning in Japanese society: Traditional birth control in a modern urban culture. Princeton, N.J.: Princeton University Press.

Cook, Alice H. and H. Hayashi. 1980. Working women in Japan. Ithaca: New York State School of Industrial and Labor Relations.

Cornell, John. 1964. Dōzoku: An example of evolution and transition in Japanese village society. Comparative study in sociology and history, vol. 6.

Cornell, Laurel L. 1981a. Paternal death and heir's age at marriage in Tokugawa Japan. Paper presented at the Social Science History Association Annual Meeting, October 23-25, Nashville, Tennessee.

Cornell, Laurel L. 1981b. Peasant family and inheritance in a Japanese community, 1671 - 1980: An anthropological analysis of local population registers. Ph.D. diss., Johns Hopkins University.

Cornell, Laurel L. 1983. Retirement, inheritance, and intergenerational conflict in preindustrial Japan. Journal of Family History 8:55-69.

Crawcour, Sidney. 1961. Documentary sources of Tokugawa economic and social history. Journal of Asian Studies 20:345-351.

Dore, Ronald P. 1958. City life in Japan: A study of a Tokyo ward. Berkeley: University of California Press.

Dore, Ronald P. 1965. Education in Tokugawa Japan. Berkeley: University of California Press.

Elder, Glen, Jr. 1977. Family history and the life course. Journal of Family History 4:279-304.

Eng, Robert Y. and Thomas C. Smith. 1975-76. Peasant families and population control in 18th century Japan. Journal of Interdisciplinary History 6:417-445.

Fruin, W. Mark. 1973. Farm family migration: The case of Echizen in the nineteenth century. Keio Economic Studies 10(2):37-46.

Fruin, W. Mark. 1980. The family as a firm and the firm as a family in Japan: The case of Kikkoman Shoyu Company Limited. Journal of Family History 5(4):432-449.

Fruin, W. Mark. 1983. Kikkoman: Company, clan and community. Cambridge, Mass.: Harvard University Press.

Fujiki, Norio. 1972. The koseki as a source for genetic studies. In Studies in Asian Geneology. Spencer J. Palmer, ed. Provo, Utah: Brigham Young University Press.

Fujimoto, Takeshi. 1978. Nihonjin no raifu saikuru (The life cycle of the Japanese). Tokyo: Rodo Kagaku Kenkyusho (Labor Science Institute).

Fukushima, Masao, ed. 1977. Kazoku: Seisaku to ho 3, Sengo Nihon kazoku no doko (Family: Policy and law 3, trends in the post-war Japanese family). Tokyo: University of Tokyo Press.

Fukushima, Masao. 1967. Nihon shihon shugi to ie seido (Japanese capitalism and the Japanese family system). Tokyo: University of Tokyo Press.

Fukutake, Tadashi. 1967. Japanese rural society. Translated by Ronald P. Dore. Ithaca, N.Y.: Cornell University Press.

Furushima, Toshio. 1949. Kazoku keitai to nogyo no hattatsu (Family form and the development of agriculture). Tokyo: Gakusei Shobo.

Fuse, Akiko. 1967. Tōshikazoku no Naibu Kōzō no Henyō ni Kansuru Ichikōsatsu. Shakaigaku Hyōron (Japanese Sociological Review) 68:45-71. Translated as Role structure of dual career families. Journal of Comparative Family Studies 12(3):329-336. Special Issue, Summer 1981.

Fuse, Akiko. 1977. Review of Ie to gendai kazoku, Morioka Kiyomi and Yamane Tsuneo, eds. Shakaigaku Hyōron (Japanese Sociological Review) 27(4): 77-80.

Fuse, Akiko. 1981. See Fuse 1967.

Fuse, Akiko and Matsuura Isao. 1977. Rōdōsha kazoku no seikatsushi: Seika no iji o chūshin ni mita jirei kenkyū (The life history of working class family: A case study on income development). Sapporo Shōka Daigaku Ronshu, pt. 1:21:1-22.

Goode, William J. 1963. World revolution and family patterns. New York: Free Press.

Hagestad, Gunhild O. and Bernice L. Neugarten. 1985. Age and the life course. In Handbook of aging and the social sciences, 2nd ed. Robert H. Binstock and Ethel Shanas, eds. New York: Van Nostrand Reinhold Co.

Hall, John W. 1975. Rule by status in Tokugawa Japan. Journal of Japanese Studies 1(1):37-49.

Hamaguchi, Eshun. 1985. The career patterns of the Japanese. In Family and life course of middle-aged men. Morioka Kiyomi, ed. Tokyo: Family and Life Course Study Group.

Hane, Mikiso. 1982. Peasants, rebels and outcasts: The underside of modern Japan. New York: Pantheon Books.

Hanley, Susan B. 1972. Toward an analysis of demographic and economic change in Tokugawa Japan. Journal of Asian Studies 31:515-537.

Hanley, Susan B. 1973. Migration and economic change in Okayama during the Tokugawa period. Keio Economic Studies 10(2):19-36.

Hanley, Susan B. 1974. Fertility, mortality, and life expectancy in pre-modern Japan. Population Studies 38(1):127-141.

Hanley, Susan. 1985. Family and fertility in four Tokugawa villages. In Family and population in east Asian history. Susan Hanley and Arthur Wolf, eds. Stanford: Stanford University Press.

Hanley, Susan and Arthur Wolf, eds. 1985. Family and population in east Asian history. Stanford: Stanford University Press.

Hanley, Susan B. and Arthur P. Wolf. In preparation. Historical demography and family history in east Asia (tentative title).

Hanley, Susan B. and Yamamura Kozo. 1971. A quiet transformation in Tokugawa economic history. Journal of Asian Studies 30:373-384.

Hanley, Susan B. and Yamamura Kozo. 1977. Economic and demographic change in preindustrial Japan, 1600 - 1868. Princeton, N.J.: Princeton University Press.

Harada, Takashi. 1978. Changes of family types and the care of old people in the homes. Shakaigaku Hyoron (Japanese Sociological Review) 29(1): 50-66.

Haraguchi, Torao, et al. 1975. Status system and social organization of Satsuma. Tokyo: University of Tokyo Press.

Hardacre, Helen. 1984. Lay Buddhism in contemporary Japan: Reiyukai Kyodan. Princeton, N.J.: Princeton University Press.

Hareven, Tamara. 1982a. American families in transition: Historical perspectives on change. In Normal family processes. Froma Walsh, ed. New York: The Guilford Press.

Hareven, Tamara. 1982b. The life course and aging in historical perspective. In Aging and life course transitions: An interdisciplinary perspective. Tamara Hareven and Kathleen J. Adams, eds. New York: The Guilford Press.

Hasegawa, Akihiko. 1981. Rojin to kazoku (The elderly and the family). In Nihonjin no kazoku kankei (Japanese family relations). Kamiko Takeji and Masuda Kokichi eds. Toyko: Yuhikaku.

Hasegawa, Noriko. 1984. Nisetai senyo jutaku ni okeru musuko fufu dokyo oyobi musume fufu dokyo no tokusei (Characteristics of co-residence with married son in household designed for two families and with married daughter in single-family household). Ronen Shakai Kagaku 2:91-106.

Hayama, Teisaku. 1981. Hokenteki shonomin keiei no bunritsuki ni okeru kazoku keitai (Family form in the timing of independence of feudal small farm management. Kazoku Shi Kenkyu 3:20-40.

Hayami, Akira. 1967. The population at the beginning of the Tokugawa period: An introduction to the historical demography of pre-industrial Japan. Keio Economic Studies 4:1-28.

Hayami, Akira. 1968a. The demographic analysis of a village in Tokugawa Japan: Kandoshinden of Owari province, 1778-1871. Keio Economic Studies 5:50-88.

Hayami, Akira. 1968b. Kinsei Shinshu Suwa chiho no jinko susei (Population trends in Suwa County). Mita Gakkai Zasshi 6:2.

Hayami, Akira. 1969. Aspects demographiques d'un village Japonois 1671 - 1871. Annales E.S.C. 24:617-639.

Hayami, Akira. 1971. Tokugawa koki jinko hendo no chiikiteki tokusei (Regional characteristics of population change in the last part of the Tokugawa period). Mita Gakki Zasshi 64(8):67-80.

Hayami, Akira. 1973a. Kinsei noson no rekishi jinkogakuteki kenkyu (Demographic analysis of pre-modern rural village in Japan).

Hayami, Akira. 1973b. Labor migration in a pre-industrial society: A study
tracing the life histories of the inhabitants of a village. Keio Economic Studies 10(2):1-18.

Hayami, Akira. 1975. Jinkō to keizai (Population and the economy). Sūryō
keizaishi nyūmon (Introduction to quantitative economic history). H.
Shimbo, A. Hayami, and S. Nishikawa, eds. Tokyo: Nihon Hyōronsha.

Hayami, Akira. 1979. Thank you Francis Xavier: An essay in the use of micro-
data for historical demography of Tokugawa Japan. Keio Economic Studies
16(1-2):65-81.

Hayami, Akira. 1980a. Class differences in marriage and fertility among
Tokugawa villagers in Mino province. Translated by Laurel L. Cornell.
Keio Economic Studies 17(1):1-17.

Hayami, Akira. 1980b. Illegitimacy in Japan. In Bastardy and its comparative history. Peter Laslett, Karla Oosterveen, and Richard M. Smith,
eds. Cambridge, Mass: Harvard University Press.

Hayami, Akira. 1983. The myth of primogeniture and impartible inheritance in
Tokugawa Japan. Journal of Family History 8:3-29.

Hayami, Akira. 1985. Rural migration and fertility in Tokugawa Japan: The
village of Nishijo, 1773-1871. In Family and population in east Asian
history. Susan Hanley and Arthur Wolf, eds. Stanford: Stanford
University Press.

Hayami, Akira and Uchida Nobuko. 1972. Size of household in a Japanese county throughout the Tokugawa era. In Household and family in past time.
Peter Laslett, ed. Cambridge: Cambridge University Press.

Henderson, Dan F. 1975. Village contracts in Tokugawa Japan. Seattle:
University of Washington Press.

Hendry, Joy. 1981. Marriage in changing Japan. New York: St. Martin's
Press.

Himeoka, Tsutomu. 1983. Kazoku shakaigaku ronshū (Essays in family sociology). Tokyo: Mineruva Shobō.

Himeoka, Tsutomu, Kamiko Takeji, and Masuda Kōkichi, eds. 1974. Gendai no
shitsuke to oyako kankei-shakai kaisō, seikatsu ishiki ni yoru chōsa to
bunseki (Socialization practices and parent-child relationships today in
terms of social class and life consciousness). Tokyo: Kawashima Shoten.

Hiraya, Noburu. 1972. The extent and preservation of original historical
records in Japan. In Studies in Asian geneology. Spencer J. Palmer, ed.
Provo, Utah: Brigham Young University Press.

Hogan, Dennis. 1981. Transitions and social change: The early lives of
American men. New York: Academic Press.

Hosoda, Morio. 1976. Shitsuke fuan no kazokuteki haikei (Family background
of insecurity regarding child-rearing). Kazoku Kenkyu Nenpo (Annals of
Family Studies) 2:17-30.

Hosoe, Yoko. 1980. Rōnengo fūfu no seikatsu tekiō (Life adjustment for the post-retirement couple). Rōnen Shakai Kagaku (Japanese Journal of Gerontology) 2:126-181.

Iga, Mitsuya. 1978. Fujin shūgyō no shūki-teki henka to rekishi-teki henka (Cyclical variations and historical tendencies of women's working). Shakaigaku Hyōron (Japanese Sociological Review) 29(3):37-56.

Iida, Tetsuya. 1976. Kazoku no shakaigaku (Family sociology). Tokyo: Mineruva Shobō.

Ishihara, Kunio. 1976. Setaishu kengen no setaiteki idō (General transfer of household directorship). In Ie to gendai kazoku. Morioka Kiyomi and Yamane Tsuneo, eds. Tokyo: Baifūkan.

Ishihara, Kunio. 1977. Setai shusaiken kara mita raifu saikuru to kazoku hendō. In Gendai kazoku no raifu saikuru. Morioka Kiyomi, ed. Tokyo: Baifūkan.

Translated as Trends in the generational continuity and succession to household directorship. Journal of Comparative Family Studies 12(3): 351-364. Special Issue, Summer 1981.

Ishihara, Kunio. 1981a. See Ishihara 1977.

Ishihara, Kunio. 1981b. Forerunners of life course studies in Japan. U.S.-Japan comparisons on the family and the life course. Unpublished ms.

Ishihara, Kunio. 1981c. Review of Onna yakuwari (Female roles), by Yoriko Meguro. Kazoku Kenkyū Nenpō (Annals of Family Studies) 7:83-86.

Ishihara, Kunio. 1982. Sengo Nihon no kazoku ishiki (Opinions about the Family in Postwar Japan). Kazokushi Kenkyū 6:118-139.

Ishihara, Kunio. n.d.a. Kin-family career of immigrants from the rural stem family in transition. Unpublished ms.

Ishihara, Kunio. n.d.b. Social stress and mental health in a Japanese urbanized city. Unpublished ms.

Ishihara, Kunio, et al. 1985. Intergenerational family careers in the historical context. In Family and life course of middle-aged men. Morioka Kiyomi, ed. Tokyo: Family and Life Course Study Group.

Ishii, Rōsuke. 1980. Nihon sōzokuhō shi (The history of succession law in Japan). Tokyo: Sobunsha.

Iwagami, Mami. 1976. Tōshi shinzoku kenkyū e no mondai to shiten (New perspectives and issues in the study of urban kinship). Kazoku Kenkyū Nenpō (Annals of Family Studies) 2:72-87.

Izumi no Kai, ed. 1965. Shufu no sensō taikenki (The records of the housewives' experience of the war). Nagoya: Fūbaisha.

Izumi, S. and M. Gamō. 1952. Nihon shakai no chiiki-sei (Regional differences in Japanese society). Nihon Chiri Shin Taikei 11:37-76.

Japan Institute of Labor. 1981. Problems of working women. Japanese industrial relations, series 8.

Johnson, Erwin. 1964. The stem family and its extension in present day Japan. American Anthropologist 66:839-851.

Kakizaki, Kyōichi. 1977. Setai keitai no shūkiteki ikō to itsudatsu (Cyclical shifts and deviations in household form). In Gendai kazoku no raifu saikuru. Morioka Kiyomi, ed. Tokyo: Baifukan.

Kamiko, Takeji. 1979. Kazoku yakuwari kenkyū (Study of family roles). Tokyo: Mineruva Shobo.

Kamiko, Takeji. 1981. Nihon no kazoku (The Japanese family). In Nihonjin no kazoku kankei. Kamiko Takeji and Masuda Kōkichi, eds. Tokyo: Yūhikaku.

Kamiko, Takeji. n.d.a. The inner structure of the three-generation household. Unpublished ms.

Kamiko, Takeji, et al. n.d.b. Live and values of aged couples living separate from their children and their relationships with their married son(s): An interim report. U.S.-Japan comparisons on the family and the life course. Unpublished ms.

Kamiko, Takeji and Masuda Kōkichi, eds. 1976. Sansedai kazoku: Sedaikan kankei no jisshoteki kenkyū (Three-generation families: An empirical study of generational relations. Tokyo: Kakiuchi Shuppan.

Kamiko, Takeji and Masuda Kōkichi. 1981. Nihonjin no kazoku kankei (Japanese family relationships). Tokyo: Yūhikaku.

Kamiko, Takeji and Noguchi Michihiko. 1985. On the co-residence of parents and married child. In Family and life course of middle-aged men. Morioka Kiyomi, ed. Tokyo: Family and Life Course Study Group.

Kato, Tsuyoshi. 1971. Generational differences in values and attitudes between Japanese college students and their fathers, with some implications for historical change of values. Monumenta Nipponica 26(3/4): 415-429.

Kawaai, Chieko and Inoue Katsuya. 1980. Kosodate shūryōki no jōsei no ikikata (The life of women in the post-parental period). Rōnen Shakai Kagaku (Japanese Journal of Gerontology) 2:108-125.

Kawai, Hayao. 1981. Violence in the home: Conflict between two principles -- maternal and paternal. Japan Quarterly 28(3):370-378.

Kawamoto, A. 1973. Kindai bungaku ni okeru ie no kōzō: Sono shakaigaku-teki kosatsu (The structure of ie described in modern literature: sociological implications). Shakai Shiso (Social Thought).

Kawashima, Takeyoshi and Kurt Steiner. 1961. Modernization and divorce rate trends in Japan. Economic Development and Cultural Change 9:213-239.

Kertzer, David I. 1983. Generation as a sociological problem. Annual Review of Sociology 9:125-149.

Kii, Toshi. 1979. Recent extension of retirement age in Japan. Gerontologist 19:481-486.

Kitō, Hiroshi. 1983. Nihon nisennen no jinkōshi (Two thousand years of Japanese demographic history). Tokyo: PHP Kenkyūshō.

Kitano, Seiichi and Masaoka Kanji. 1975. Shūshū (Conclusion). In Ie to shinzoku sōshiki (The ie and kinship relationships). Tokyo: Waseda Daigaku Shakai Kagaku Kenkyūshō.

Kitano, Seiichi and Okada Yuzuru, eds. 1959. Ie: Sono kōzō bunseki (Ie: Analysis of its structure). Tokyo: Sōbunsha.

Kitano, Seiichi. 1970. Dōzoku and kindred in a Japanese rural society. In Families east and west. Reuben Hill and René Konig, eds. The Hague: Mouton.

Kitano, Seiichi. 1976. Ie to dōzoku no kisō riron (Basic theories of the household and the dōzoku). Tokyo: Kaizōsha.

Kitano, Seiichi. 1962. Dōzoku and ie in Japan: The meaning of family geneological relationships. In Japanese culture: Its development and characteristics. Robert J. Smith and Richard K. Beardsley, eds. Chicago: Aldine Publishing Co.

Kito, Hiroshi. 1976. Tokugawa jidai nōson no nyūji shibō (Peasant infanticide in the Tokugawa era). Mita Gakkai Zasshi 69(8):88-95.

Kokumin Seikatsu Kenkyūshō (Social and Economic Affairs Research Institute). 1968. Setai hendō to seikatsu kōzō -- Nippon no raifu saikuru (The change of household and the structure of life -- The life cycle in Japan). Tokyo: Tōyō Keizai Shimpōsha.

Kokumin Seikatsu Sentā (Japan Consumer Information Center). 1976. Tōshi kazoku no seikatsu reki (The life history of urban families). Tokyo: Domesusha.

Komobuchi, Midori. 1972. Sanseidai kazoku no ningen kankei (Human relationships in the three-generation family). Studies of Social Problems 22(1,2):16-49.

Komobuchi, Midori. 1981. Haigūsha sentaku to kekkon (Mate selection and marriage). In Nihonjin no kazoku kankei (Japanese family relations). Kamiko Takeji and Masuda Kōkichi, eds. Tokyo: Yūhikaku.

Koyama, Takashi. 1959. Kazoku keitai no shūkiteki henka (Cyclical change in family form). In Ie: Sono kōzō bunseki. Seiichi Kitano and Okada Yuzuru, eds. Tokyo: Sōbunsha.

Translated as The pre-modern peasant family and its life cycle pattern. In Family and household in changing Japan. Journal of Comparative Family Studies 12(3):293-304. Special Issue, Summer 1981.

Koyama, Takashi. 1964. Changing family composition and the position of the aged in the Japanese family. International Journal of Comparative Sociology 5:155-161.

Koyama, Takashi. 1966. The significance of relatives at the turning point of the family system in Japan. In Japanese Sociological Studies. Paul Halmos, ed. Sociological Review Monograph. No. 10. University of Keele.

Koyama, Takashi. 1976. Kazoku hendō no rekishiteki haikei (Historical background of family change). In Ie to gendai kazoku (Household and the present day Japanese family). Morioka Kiyomi and Yamane Tsuneo, eds. Tokyo: Baifūkan.

Koyama, Takashi. 1980. Footsteps of 50 years -- Memoirs of a student of sociology. Tokyo: Ochanomizu Shobō.

Koyama, Takashi. 1981. See Koyama 1959.

Koyama, Takashi, ed. 1967. Gendai kazoku no yakuwari kōzō: Fūfu, oyako no kitai to genjitsu (Family role structure today: Expectations and performances of husband and wife, parent and child). Tokyo: Baifūkan.

Koyama, Takashi, ed. 1973. Gendai kazoku no oyako kankei: Shitsuke no shakaigakuteki bunseki (Parent-child relationships in the contemporary family: A sociological analysis of socialization practices). Tokyo: Baifūkan.

Koyama, Takashi. et al. 1960. Gendai kazoku no kenkyū: Jittai to chōsei (A study of the contemporary family: Reality and adjustment). Tokyo: Kobundō.

Koyama, Takashi, Morioka Kiyomi, and Fumie Kumagai. 1981. Family and household in changing Japan. Journal of Comparative Family Studies 12(3). Special Issue, Summer 1981.

Koyano, Shōgō. 1964. Changing family behavior in four Japanese communities. Journal of Marriage and the Family 26:149-159.

Koyano, Shōgō. 1976. Sociological studies in Japan: Family and kinship. Bibliography. Current Sociology 24(1):37-42, 109-125.

Kōsei Tōkei Kyōkai. 1982. Kokumin eisei no dōkō (Trends in public health). Kōsei no Shihyō 29(9), Special Issue.

Kumagai, Fumie and Gerald O'Donoghue. 1978. Conjugal power and conjugal violence in Japan and the U.S.A. Journal of Comparative Family Studies 9(2):211-222.

Kumagai, Fumie. 1981. Filial violence: A peculiar parent-child relationship in the Japanese family today. Journal of Comparative Family Studies 12(3):337-350. Special Issue, Summer 1981.

Kumagai, Fumie. 1983. Changing divorce in Japan. Journal of Family History 8:85-108.

Laslett, Peter. 1973. The world we have lost. 2nd ed. New York: Scribner.

Laslett, Peter. 1978. The stem-family hypothesis and its privileged position. In Statistical studies of historical social structure. Kenneth W. Wachter, Eugene A. Hammel, and Peter Laslett, eds. New York: Academic Press.

Lebra, Joyce, et al., eds. 1976. Women in changing Japan. Boulder, Colo.: Westview Press.

Lebra, Takie S. 1974. Intergenerational continuity and discontinuity in moral values among Japanese: A preliminary report. In Youth, socialization, and mental health. William P. Lebra, ed. Honolulu: University Press of Hawaii.

Lebra, Takie S. 1979. Dilemma and strategies of aging among contemporary Japanese women. Ethnology 18:337-353.

Lebra, Takie S. 1984. Japanese women: Constraint and fulfillment. Honolulu: University of Hawaii Press.

Lock, Margaret. 1986. Plea for acceptance: School refusal syndrome in Japan. Social Science and Medicine 23:99-112.

Long, Susan O. 1980. Fame, fortune, and friends: Constraints and strategies in the careers of Japanese physicians. Ph.D. diss., Urbana: University of Illinois.

Long, Susan O. 1986. Roles, careers, and femininity in biomedicine: Women physicians and nurses in Japan. Social Science and Medicine 22:81-90.

Maeda, Daisaku. 1977. Research in social gerontology in Japan. Social Gerontology 5:3-13.

Maeda, Daisaku. 1978. Aging in eastern society. In The social challenge of aging. David Hobman, ed. New York: St. Martin's Press.

Maeyama, Takashi. 1981. Hisōzokusha no seishin shi -- Aru Nikkei Braziljin no henreki (The mental history of a non-successor -- A Japanese Brazilian's life). Tokyo: Ochanomizu Shobo.

Makino, Tatsumi, et al. 1970. Juvenile delinquency and home training. In Families in east and west. Reuben Hill and René Konig, eds. The Hague: Mouton.

Martin, L. and S. Cutler. 1983. Mortality decline and Japanese family structure. Population and Development Review 9:633-650.

Masaoka, Kanji, et al. 1985. Turning points: A study on a qualitative change in the life course. In Family and life course of middle-aged men. Morioka Kiyomi, ed. Tokyo: Family and Life Course Study Group.

Masaoka, Kanji. 1975. Dōzoku to shinrui (Dōzoku and kindred). In Ie to shinzoku sōshiki (The ie and kinship relations). Tokyo: Waseda Daigaku Shakai Kagaku Kenkyushō.

Masaoka, Kanji. 1981a. A contribution toward a study comparing Americans and Japanese historical changes in the life course and the family (1). U.S.-Japan comparisons on the family and the life course. Unpublished ms.

Masaoka, Kanji. 1981b. Ie kenkyū no tenkai to kadai (Development of and issues in ie studies). Kazoku Shi Kenkyu (Studies in Family History) 3:68-92.

Masuda, Kōkichi. 1972a. Seiryoku kankei (Power relations). In Shakaigaku Kōza 3: Kazoku shakaigaku. Morioka Kiyomi, ed. Tokyo: University of Tokyo Press.

Masuda, Kōkichi. 1972b. Yome-shūtome kankei no henka: Tochi kinkō nōson no chōsa hōkoku. Konan Daigaku Kiyō (Bungakuhen) 9:1-19.

Translated as Bride's progress: How a yome becomes a shūtome. In Adult episodes in Japan. David W. Plath, ed. Leiden: E.J. Brill.

Masuda, Kōkichi. 1975. See Masuda 1972b.

Masuda, Kōkichi. 1981. Fūfu kankei (Conjugal relations). In Nihonjin no kazoku kankei (Japanese family relations). Kamiko Takeji and Masuda Kokichi, eds. Tokyo: Yūhikaku.

Matsubara, Jirō. 1983. Kazoku no kiki (The crisis of the family). Tokyo: Nihon Keizai Shimbunsha.

Matsumoto, Y. Scott. 1962. Notes on primogeniture in postwar Japan. In Japanese culture: Its development and characteristics. Robert J. Smith and Richard K. Beardsley, eds. Chicago: Aldine Publishing Co.

Matsumura, Kazunori. 1979. The family life cycle and working system in a single rice crop area of Japan. Shakaigaku Hyōron (Japanese Sociological Review) 30(3):61-84.

Matsunari, Megumi. 1975. Kazoku no henka-katei ni kaizai suru hauzgingu yōin (Housing as a factor affecting the process of family change), Kazoku Kenkyū Nenpō (Annals of Family Studies) 1:53-71.

Matsuo, Tsuneko. 1981. Nyuyōji to oyako kankei (Parent-child relations of infants). In Nihonjin no kazoku kankei (Japanese family relations). Kamiko Takeji and Masuda Kōkichi, eds. Tokyo: Yūhikaku.

Matsushima, Hiroko. 1983. Chūkōnen josei no rōgo ni tsuite no ishiki (Attitudes of middle-aged and elderly women toward old age). Rōnen Shakai Kagaku 5:100-113.

McClain, J. 1980. Castle towns and daimyō authority. Journal of Japanese Studies 6(2):267-299.

McMullen, I.J. 1975. Non-agnatic adoption: A Confucian controversy in 17th and 18th century Japan. Harvard Journal of Asiatic Studies 35:133-189.

Meguro, Yoriko. 1974a. Family and social network in modern Japan: A study of an urban sample. Ph.D. diss., Case Western Reserve University.

Meguro, Yoriko. 1974b. Gendai kazoku no shakaiteki nettowāku: Pasu kaiseki no ōyo (The social network of the modern family: An application of path analysis). Shakaigaku Hyōron (Japanese Sociological Review) 25(2):37-48.

Meguro, Yoriko. 1977. Kazoku nettowāku, kazoku shūki, shakaihendō -- 5 kazoku hanpuku chōsa o motoni (Family network, family life cycle, and social change -- report on segmented longitudinal panels of five families). In Gendai kazoku no raifu saikuru. Morioka Kiyomi, ed. Tokyo: Baifukan.

Meguro, Yoriko. 1978. Review of Kōreika shakai no kazoku shūki. Chūbachi Masayoshi, ed. Kazoku Kenkyu Nenpō (Annals of Family Studies) 4:88-90.

Meguro, Yoriko. 1980. Ũnna yakuwari (Female roles). Tokyo: Kakiuchi Shuppan.

Meguro, Yoriko. 1985. Effects of World War II experiences on men's lives. In Family and life course of middle-aged men. Morioka Kiyomi, ed. Tokyo: Family and Life Course Study Group.

Ministry of Health and Welfare. 1984. Annual report on health and welfare for 1983: The trend of a new era and social security. Tokyo: Japan International Corporation of Welfare Services.

Mitani, T. 1966. Gendai tōshi kazoku ni okeru sansedai fūfu dōkyō no mondai (The structure of the contemporary Japanese three-generation family). Shakaigaku Hyōron (Japanese Sociological Review) 17(1):86-100.

Mitani, Tetsuo. 1978. Kōreisha setai no kōzō ni kansuru ichikōsatsu (A study of the household structure of old people). Kazoku Kenkyu Nenpō (Annals of family studies) 4:26-37.

Mochizuki, Takashi. 1972. Haigūsha sentaku to kekkon (Mate selection and marriage). In Shakaigaku kōza 3: Kazoku shakaigaku. Morioka Kiyomi, ed. Tokyo: University of Tokyo Press.

Mochizuki, Takashi. 1976. Haigūsha sentaku no henka (Changes in mate selection). In Ie to gendai kazoku. Morioka Kiyomi and Yamane Tsuneo, eds. Tokyo: Baifūkan.

Mochizuki, Takashi. 1977. Hattatsu apurōchi kara mita haigūsha sentaku. In Gendai kazoku no raifu saikuru. Morioka Kiyomi, ed. Tokyo: Baifūkan.

Translated as Changing patterns of mate selection. Journal of Comparative Family Studies 12(3):317-328. Special Issue, Summer 1981.

Mochizuki, Takashi and Motomura Hiroshi. 1980. Gendai kazoku no kiki (Crisis in the modern family). Tokyo: Yūhikaku.

Mochizuki, Takashi, et al. 1985. Transition to adulthood in the life course. In Family and life course of middle-aged men. Morioka Kiyomi, ed. Tokyo: Family and Life Course Study Group.

Moore, Ray A. 1970. Adoption and samurai mobility in Tokugawa Japan. Journal of Asian Studies 29:617-632.

Moore, Ray A. 1972. Family records and social history in Tokugawa Japan. In Studies in Asian geneology. Spencer J. Palmer, ed. Provo, Utah: Brigham Young University Press.

Morgan, S. Philip and K. Hirosima. 1983. The persistence of extended family residence in Japan: Anachronism or alternative strategy? American Sociological Review 48:269-281.

Morgan, S. Philip, et al. 1984. Modern fertility patterns: Contrasts between the United States and Japan. Population and Development Review 10:19-40.

Morioka, Kiyomi. 1964. A critical review of studies in the family life cycle. Kokusai Kirisutokyō Daigaku Shakai Kagaku Jānaru (International Christian University Social Science Journal), no. 5. Translated by Y.H. Kim, in unpublished ms.

Morioka, Kiyomi. 1967a. Kazoku Shakaigaku (Family sociology). Tokyo: Yuhikaku.

Morioka, Kiyomi. 1967b. Life cycle patterns in Japan, China, and the U.S. Journal of Marriage and the Family 29(3):595-606.

Morioka, Kiyomi. 1972. Shakaigaku kōza 3: Kazoku shakaigaku (Sociology Lecture 3: Family Sociology). Tokyo: University of Tokyo Press.

Morioka, Kiyomi. 1973. Kazoku shūki ron (Family Cycles). Tokyo: Baifūkan.

Chapter 4 translated as Family and housing over the life cycle. Journal of Comparative Family Studies 12(3):365-396. Special Issue, Summer 1981.

Morioka, Kiyomi. 1974. Industrialization, family ideologies, and demographic factors in family change in contemporary Japan. International Journal of Sociology of the Family 4:148-160.

Morioka, Kiyomi. 1981a. The development of family sociology in Japan. Journal of Comparative Family Studies 12(3):i-iii. Special Issue: Family and household changing Japan, Summer 1981.

Morioka, Kiyomi. 1981b. See Morioka 1973.

Morioka, Kiyomi. 1981c. Multi-generation researches in Japan and potentials for the U.S.-Japan cooperative study in the family and the life course. Unpublished ms.

Morioka, Kiyomi. 1984a. Ie no hembō to senzo no matsuri (Ancestor worship and the transformation of the household). Tokyo: Nihon Kirisuto Kyōdan Shuppankyoku.

Morioka, Kiyomi. 1984b. Nichijō seikatsu ni okeru shihika (Privatization in daily life). Shakaigaku Hyōron (Japanese Sociological Review) 34: 130-137.

Morioka, Kiyomi. 1984c. Koyama Takashi Sensei o shinonde (Remembering Professor Takashi Koyama). Shakaigaku Hyōron 34:452-455.

Morioka, Kiyomi, ed. 1977. Gendai kazoku no raifu saikuru (The life cycle of the modern family). Tokyo: Baifūkan.

Morioka, Kiyomi, ed. 1985. Family and life course of middle-aged men. Tokyo: Family and Life Course Study Group.

Morioka, Kiyomi and Kazuo Aoi, eds. Raifu cōsu to sedai (The life course and generation). Tokyo: Kakiuchi Shuppan, in press.

Morioka, Kiyomi and Yamane Tsuneo. eds. 1976. Ie to gendai kazoku (Household and the present day Japanese family). Tokyo: Baifūkan.

Morioka, Kiyomi, et al. 1968. Tokyo kinkō danchi kazoku no seikatsushi to shakai sanka (The life history and social participation of families in an apartment complex near Tokyo). Kokusai Kirisutokyō Daigaku Shakai Kagaku Janaru (International Christian University Social Science Journal), no. 7.

Morioka, Kiyomi, et al. 1985. Intergenerational relations: Generational differences and changes. In Family and life course of middle-aged men. Morioka Kiyomi, ed. Tokyo: The Family and Life Course Study Group.

Morita, Masahiro. 1979. Yanagita Kunio no kazokuron (On Yanagita's theory of family). Kazoku Kenkyū Nenpō (Annals of Family Studies) 5:50-62.

Morris, Dana and Thomas C. Smith. 1985. Fertility and mortality in an outcast village in Japan, 1750-1869. In Family and population in east Asian history. Susan Hanley and Arthur Wolf, eds. Stanford: Stanford University Press.

Morris, Dana and Stephen Vlastos. 1980. Review of Economic and demographic change in pre-industrial Japan, 1600 - 1868, by Susan Hanley and Kozo Yamamura. Journal of Asian Studies 39(2):361-368.

Mosk, Carl. 1977. Demographic transition in Japan. Journal of Economic History 37:655-674.

Mosk, Carl. 1978. Fecundity, infanticide, and food consumption in Japan. Explorations in Economic History 15:269-289.

Mosk, Carl. 1979. The decline of marital fertility in Japan. Population Studies 33:19-38.

Mosk, Carl. 1980. Nuptiality in Meiji Japan. Journal of Social History 13:474-489.

Mosk, Carl. 1981a. The evolution of the pre-modern demographic regime in Japan. Population Studies 35:28-52.

Mosk, Carl. 1981b. Fertility and occupation. Social Science History 5:293-315.

Mosk, Carl. 1983. Patriarchy and fertility: Japan and Sweden, 1880-1960. New York: Academic Press.

Nagai, Michio. 1953. Dōzoku: A preliminary study of the Japanese "extended family" group and its social and economic functions (based on the researches of K. Aruga). Interim Report no. 7. Columbus: Ohio State University Research Foundation.

Naikaku Sōri Daijin Kanbō Rōjin Taisaku Shitsu (Prime Minister's Office, Elderly Policy Section). 1975. Rōjin fuyō ni kansuru chōsa (A survey of elderly support). Tokyo.

Naito, Kanji. 1968. Kinsei shōki Nagasaki no kazoku dōtai (Family dynamics in Nagasaki City, 17th century). Shakaigaku Hyōron (Japanese Sociological Review) 73:83-104.

Nakagawa, Zennosuke, et al., eds. 1955. Kazoku mondai to kazoku hō (Family problems and family law), 6 vols.

Nakamura, James I. 1981. Human capital accumulation in pre-modern rural Japan. Journal of Economic History 41(2):263-279.

Nakamura, James I. and Miyamoto Matao. 1982. Social structure and population change: A comparative study of Tokugawa Japan and Ch'ing China. Economic Development and Cultural Change 30:229-270.

Nakane, Chie. 1967. Kinship and economic organization in rural Japan. London: The Athlone Press.

Nakane, Chie. 1972. An interpretation of the size and structure of the household in Japan over three centuries. In Household and family in past time. Peter Laslett, ed. Cambridge: Cambridge University Press.

Nakane, Chie. 1974. Cultural anthropology in Japan. Annual Review of Anthropology 3:57-73.

Nakano, Takashi. 1962. Recent studies of change in the Japanese family. International Social Science Journal 14:527-538.

Nakano, Takashi. 1977. Kōjutsu no seikatsu shi: Aru onna no ai to urami no Nihon kindai (A life history by aural personal document: A woman's love and hatred reflecting modern Japan). Tokyo: Ochanomizu Shobō.

Nakano, Takashi. 1981. Ritō Tokara ni ikita otoko (A man who lived in Tokara, an isolated island). Tokyo: Ochanomizu Shobō.

Nakano, Takashi. 1982. On the sociological research of the individual. Shakaigaku Hyōron (Japanese Sociological Review) 32(4):127.

Naoi, Michiko. 1979. Toshibu ni okeru kazoku fuyō no henka (Changes in family support in a metropolitan area). Rōnen Shakai Kagaku (Japanese Journal of Gerontology) 1:31-36.

Napier, Ronald. 1984. Review of Patriarchy and fertility by Carl Mosk. Journal of Asian Studies 43:767-769.

Narimatsu, Saeko. 1985. Kinsei Tōhoku nōson no hitobito (Tohoku villagers of early modern times). Tokyo: Mineruva Shobō.

Nasu, Sōichi and Masuda Kōkichi, eds. 1972. Rōjin to kazoku no shakaigaku (Sociological studies on the elderly and the family). Nihon no Rōjin, vol. 3 (The elderly in Japan) vol. 3. Tokyo: Kakiuchi Shuppan.

Nasu, Sōichi and Yuzawa Yasuhiko, eds. 1970. Rōjin fuyō no kenkyū (Studies on the support of the elderly). Tokyo: Kakiuchi Shuppan.

NHK Institute of Public Opinion. 1976. Graphic presentation of Japanese time budget. Tokyo: Japan Broadcast Publication.

NHK. 1981. "Nichibei hikaku" chōsa ("Japan-U.S. comparison" survey). Seron Chōsa (July):27-43.

Nihon Ishikai (Japan Medical Association). 1977. Kokumin iryō nenkan (People's health yearbook). Tokyo: Shinshūsha.

- 109 -

Noda, Yoko. 1983 . Characteristic features of "Ikigai" in old age (abstract). Rōnen Shakai Kagaku 5:128.

Nojiri, Yoriko. See entries under Meguro, Yoriko.

Nomura, Tetsuya. 1976a. Seiryoku kankei (Power relations). In Sansedai kazoku. Kamiko Takeji and Masuda Kōkichi, eds. Tokyo: Kakiuchi Shuppan.

Nomura, Tetsuya. 1976b. Shōnen to haigūsha sentaku (Youth and mate selection). In Ie to gendai kazoku. Morioka Kiyomi and Yamane Tsuneo, eds. Tokyo: Baifūkan.

Nomura, Tetsuya. 1981. Shishunki no ko to oyako kankei (Parent-child relations of adolescents). In Nihonjin no kazoku kankei (Japanese family relations). Kamiko Takeji and Masuda Kōkichi, eds. Tokyo: Yūhikaku.

Norbeck, Edward. 1954. Takashima: A Japanese fishing community. Salt Lake City: University of Utah Press.

Norbeck, Edward. 1978. Country to city: The urbanization of a Japanese hamlet. Salt Lake City: University of Utah Press.

Ōhashi, Kaoru and Shimizu Shinji. 1972. Tōshi ni okeru shinzoku kankei no ichikōsatsu -- Kawasakishi S. Shōgakko no Baai (A study of kinship relations in the city -- the case of S. school district, Kawasaki). Meiji Gakuin Ronsō 195:1-34.

Ōhbuchi, Hiroshi. 1976. Demographic transition in the process of Japanese industrialization. In Japanese industrialization and its social consequences. Hugh Patrick, ed. Berkeley: University of California Press.

Oikawa, Hiroshi. 1980. Kazoku shi kenkyū no sōkan (A new publication, Studies in Family History). Kazoku Kenkyū Nenpo 6:89-92.

Oikawa, Hiroshi. 1984. Kazoku keitai no kokusai hikaku (International comparison of family form). Rōnen Shakai Kagaku 6:51-65.

Ōishi, Shinzaburō. 1968. Kinsei sonraku no kōzō to ie seido (The structure of the pre-modern village and the ie system). Tokyo: Ochanomizu Shobō.

Ōishi, Shinzaburō. 1981. Tokugawa Shōgunke no sōzoku seido, (Succession in the Tokugawa Shogun's family). Kazoku Shi Kenkyū (Studies in Family History) 3:5-19.

Okamura, Masu. 1976. Tōhoku sanson ni miru inkyōsei no idō (Changes in the retirement system of a mountain village in northeastern Japan). In Ie to gendai kazoku. Morioka Kiyomi and Yamane Tsuneo, eds. Tokyo: Baifūkan.

Okamura, Masu. 1977. Kazoku shūki kara mita inkyō kankō no dōtai (The dynamics of retirement in view of the family life cycle). In Gendai kazoku no raifu saikuru. Morioka Kiyomi, ed. Tokyo: Baifukan.

Okayama, Masamori 1984. Rōnenki ni okeru kazoku keitai (Family form among the elderly). Rōnen Shakai Kagaku 6:15-36.

Okazaki, Yōichi. 1977. Kōreika shakai e no tenkan -- Nihon no jinko, keizai, shakai (Transition to an aging society -- Japan's population, economic, and society). Tokyo: Kōbunsha.

Osako, Masako M. 1979. Aging and family among Japanese Americans: The role of ethnic tradition in the adjustment to old age. Gerontologist 19:448-455.

Ushima, Harry T. 1983. The industrial and demographic transitions in east Asia. Population and Development Review 9:583-608.

Ōshima, Mario. 1978. Kinsei ni okeru mura to ie no shakai kōzō (The social structure of the ie and the village in the Middle Ages). Tokyo: Uchanomizu Shobo.

Ōshima, Mario. 1981. Kinsei no mura ni okeru kakōsei shihai to honke-bunke kankei (Honke-bunke relations and the distribution of independent households in the pre-modern agricultural village). Kazoku Shi Kenkyū (Studies in Family History) 3:41-67.

Palmore, Erdman. 1975. The honorable elders. Durham, N.C.: Duke University Press.

Pharr, Susan. 1981. Political women in Japan: The search for a place in political life. Berkeley: University of California Press.

Plath, David W. 1972. Japan: The after years. In Aging and modernization. D. Cowgill and L. Holmes, eds. New York: Appleton-Century-Crofts.

Plath, David W. 1980. Long engagements: Maturity in modern Japan. Stanford: Stanford University Press.

Plath, David W. 1981. Transitions and transactions: Mobilization for life course tasks. Unpublished ms.

Plath, David W. 1982. Arcs, circles, and spheres: Scheduling selfhood. Presented at the Midwest Regional Seminar on Japan, April, Earlham College, Richmond, Indiana.

Plath, David W., ed. 1975. Adult episodes in Japan. Leiden: E.J. Brill.

Plath, David W., ed. 1983. Work and lifecourse in Japan. Albany: State University of New York Press.

Robins-Mowry, Dorothy. 1983. The hidden sun: Women of modern Japan. Boulder, Colo.: Westview Press.

Rohlen, Thomas P. 1976. The promise of adulthood in Japanese spiritualism. In Adulthood. Erik Erikson, ed. New York: W.W. Norton.

Saito, Kazuko. 1977. Research on the relationship between aging and social adjustment. In Annual report on mental health 1977. Tokyo: National Institute of Mental Health.

Saito, Kazuko and Kato Masaaki. 1977. On the evaluation of the factors connected with adjustment of the aged. In Annual report on mental health 1977. Tokyo: National Institute of Mental Health.

Saito, Osamu. 1973. Migration and the labor market in Japan 1872 - 1920: A regional study. Keio Economic Studies 10(2):47-60.

Saito, Usamu. 1983. Population and the peasant family economy in proto-industrial Japan. Journal of Family History 8:30-54.

Saito, Usamu. 1984. Review of Patriarchy and fertility by Carl Mosk. Journal of Japanese Studies 10:495-504.

Saito, Yoshio. 1979. Rōjin no kazoku fuyō to shakai hendō (Family support for the aged and social change -- a survey of the Tōhoku district). Rōnen Shakai Kagaku (Japanese Journal of Gerontology) 1:37-44.

Sangyō Kenkyūshō (Housing Industry Research Institute). 1980. Jūtaku no sumikae jittai oyobi shōrai mitōshi narabi ni jūtaku sangyō ni okeru tekisetsu na taiōsaku no kentō, gaiyō (Research on the state and future outlook of changing residences and appropriate policy for the housing industry summary). Tokyo.

Sasaki, Yōichirō. 1967. Tokugawa tōshi jinko no kenkyū (Study of Tokugawa urban populations). Shikai 40.

Sasaki, Yōichirō. 1969. Hida no kuni Takayama no jinkō kenkyū (Population studies of Hida County, Takayama). In Keizaishi ni okeru jinkō (Population in economic history). Tokyo: Shakai Keizaishi Gakkai.

Sasaki, Yōichirō. 1985. Urban migration and fertility in Tokugawa Japan: The City of Takayama, 1773-1871. In Family and population in east Asian history. Susan Hanley and Arthur Wolf, eds. Stanford: Stanford University Press.

Sashida, Ryūichi. 1981. Otto no tsuzukigara ni yoru kazoku nettowāku no sai (Filial status of husbands and variation of family network). Kazoku Kenkyū Nenpō (Annals of Family Studies) 7:48-63.

Satake, Hiroto. 1977. Kazoku shūki to funsō fūfu no seikatsu (Family cycle and marital strife). In Gendai kazoku no raifu saikuru. Morioka Kiyomi, ed. Tokyo: Baifūkan.

Sekiyama, Naotarō. 1958. Kinsei Nihon no jinko kōzō (Demographic structure of early modern Japan). Tokyo.

Shimizu, Hiroaki. 1984. Kazoku, setai kōsei no chiikisa (Regional variation in family and household composition). Rōnen Shakai Kagaku 6:37-50.

Smith, Robert J. 1956. Kurusu: A Japanese agricultural community. In Two Japanese villages, by John B. Cornell and Robert J. Smith. Occasional Papers No. 5:1-112. Ann Arbor: University of Michigan Center for Japanese Studies.

Smith, Robert J. 1972. Small families, small households, and residential instability: Town and city in "pre-modern" Japan. In Household and family in past time. Peter Laslett, ed. Cambridge: Cambridge University Press.

Smith, Robert J. 1974. Ancestor worship in contemporary Japan. Stanford: Stanford University Press.

Smith, Robert J. 1978a. The domestic cycle in selected commoner families in urban Japan: 1757 - 1858. Journal of Family History 3:219-235.

Smith, Robert J. 1978b. Kurusu: The price of progress in a Japanese village, 1951 - 1975. Stanford: Stanford University Press.

Smith, Robert J. 1983. Making village women into "good wives and wise mothers" in prewar Japan. Journal of Family History 8:70-84.

Smith, Robert J. 1985. Transformations of commoner households in Tennōjimura, 1757-1858. In Family and population in east Asian history. Susan B. Hanley and Arthur P. Wolf, eds. Stanford: Stanford University Press.

Smith, Robert J. and Ella Lury Wiswell. 1982. The women of Suye Mura. Chicago: University of Chicago Press.

Smith, Thomas C. 1959. The agrarian origins of modern Japan. Stanford: Stanford University Press.

Smith, Thomas C. 1969. Farm family by-employment in pre-industrial Japan. Journal of Economic History 29(4):687-715.

Smith, Thomas C. 1977. Nakahara: Family farming and population in a Japanese village, 1717 - 1830. Stanford: Stanford University Press.

Sodei, Takako. 1977. Review of Sansedai kazoku, Kamiko Takeji and Kōkichi Masuda, eds. Shakaigaku Hyōron (Japanese Sociological Review) 28(1): 93-96.

Sodei, Takako. 1978. Review of Tōshi kazoku no seikatsureki, by Kokumin Seikatsu Sentā. Kazoku Kenkyū Nenpō (Annals of Family Studies) 4:91-94.

Soliday, Gerald. 1980. History of the family and kinship: A select international bibliography. Kraus International Publications.

Sōrifu Hōkokushitsu. 1982. Nyūyōji kyōiku. (The education of young children). Seron Chōsa (October):25-47.

Sōrifu Hōkokushitsu. 1985. Sedaikan no ishikisa (Generational differences of opinion). Seron Chōsa (May):20-23.

Sōrifu Rōjin Taisakushitsu. 1982. Rōgo no seikatsu to kaigo (Old age daily life and supports). Seron Chōsa (November):44-73.

Steiner, Kurt. 1950. Review of the civil code of Japan: Provisions affecting the family. Far Eastern Quarterly 9:169-184.

Suenari, Michio. 1972. First child inheritance in Japan. Ethnology 11: 122-126.

Sugaya, Yoshiko. 1980. Kazoku no raifu sutēji to tsuma no daiichiji kankei keisei (Family life stages and the formation of primary relations among wives in a newly developed residential area). Kazoku Kenkyū Nenpō (Annals of Family Studies) 6:42-59.

Sugioka, Naoto. 1978. Life cycle of rural families and cooperative groups. Shakaigaku Hyōron (Japanese Sociological Review) 28(3):2-27.

Sussman, Marvin B. and James C. Romeis. 1981. Family supports for the aged: A comparison of United States and Japan resources. Journal of Comparative Family Studies 12: 475-492.

Sussman, Marvin B. and James C. Romeis. 1982. Willingness to assist one's elderly parents: Responses from United States and Japan. Human Organization 41:256-259.

Taeuber, Irene B. 1958. The population of Japan. Princeton, New Jersey: Princeton University Press.

Taeuber, Irene B. 1960. Urbanization and population change in the development of modern Japan. Economic Development and Cultural Change 9:1-28.

Takahashi, Hiroko. 1980. Tōshi ni okeru kōreisha fuyō (Support of the urban elderly). Kateika Kyōiku (Home Economics Education) (September): 24-28.

Takahashi, Kumiko. 1976. Kangōfu kazoku ni okeru yakuwari chōsei no mondai (The problem of role adjustment in nurses' families). Kazoku Kenkyū Nenpō (Annals of Family Studies) 2:31-44.

Takai, Masaomi and Nakao Hidetoshi. 1977. Osakafū kinkō nōka sōzoku no genjō to mondai (The realities and problems of farm succession in suburban Osaka). In Kazoku: Seisaku to hō 3, Sengo Nihon kazoku no dōkō. Fukushima Masao, ed. Tokyo: University of Tokyo Press.

Tamura, K., ed. 1970. Gendai kazoku kankeigaku (The study of contemporary family relationships). Tokyo: Kobunsha.

Tokuoka, Hideo. 1981. Rikon to kodomo (Children and divorce). In Nihonjin no kazoku kankei (Japanese family relations). Kamiko Takeji and Masuda Kokichi, eds. Tokyo: Yūhikaku.

Tokyo Daigaku Kōkai Kōza. 1968. Ie (Ie). No. 11. Tokyo: University of Tokyo Press.

Tokyo Kyōiku Daigaku Shakaigaku Kenkyūshitsu. 1967. Nisedai hikakuhō ni yoru shakai hendo no kenkyu: Yamanashiken Katsunumachō chōsa hōkoku (A study of the social change by using two-generational comparison approach: Report on Katsunumacho, Yamanashi prefecture). Tokyo: Tokyo Kyōiku Daigaku.

Toshitani, Nobuyoshi. 1979. Family policy and family law in modern Japan. Annals of the Institute of Social Science, University of Tokyo 20:95-125.

Tsubouchi, Yoshihiro and Maeda Naribumi. 1977. Kakukazoku saikō (Rethinking the nuclear family). Tokyo: Kobundō.

Tsubouchi, Yoshihiro and Maeda Naribumi. 1980. Kakukazoku saikō shohyō ni kotaeru (A response to the review of "rethinking the nuclear family"). Shakaigaku Hyōron (Japanese Sociological Review) 30(4):109-110.

Tsuchida, Hideo. 1976. Inkyō kankō to fukusetaisei kazoku (Retirement practices and the multi-generation family system). In Ie to gendai kazoku. Morioka Kiyomi and Yamane Tsuneo, eds. Tokyo: Baifūkan.

Tsurumi, Kazuko. 1970. Social change and the individual. Princeton, N.J.: Princeton University Press.

Tsurumi, Kazuko. 1982. Review of Kōjutsu no seikatsushi: Aru onna no ai to urami no Nihon kindai, by Nakano Takashi. Shakaigaku Hyōron (Japanese Sociological Review) 32(4):73-75.

Uno, Kimiko, 1976. "Sofubo to mago" no kūkan bunri to setchoku genkan (Spatial distance as a factor in the quality of interaction between grandparents and grandchildren). Kazoku Kenkyū Nenpō (Annals of Family Studies) 2:45-58.

Uno, Masamichi. 1978a. Shakai hendōka ni okeru chihō shōtōshi kazoku no seikatsureki (Family life career in a small town under the great social change). In Kazoku shūki to sedaikan kankei (Family Life Cycle and Intergenerational Relations). Chubachi Masayoshi, ed. Tokyo: Shiseidō.

Uno, Masamichi. 1978b. Tōda kazokuron ni okeru seikatsu no shiten (The concept of "life" in Tōda's theory of the family). Kazoku Kenkyū Nenpō (Annals of Family Studies) 4:38-49.

Verdon, Michael. 1983. The stem family: Toward a general theory. In The American family in social-historical perspective, 3rd ed. Michael Gordon, ed. New York: St. Martin's Press.

Vogel, Suzanne. 1978. Professional housewife: The career of urban middle class Japanese women. Japan Interpreter 12:16-43.

Wada, Shuichi. 1981. Occupational mobility as a condition of later life adjustment. Paper presented at The 12th International Congress of Gerontology, Hamburg, W. Germany, July.

Watanabe, Yōzō. 1963. The family and the law: The individualistic premise and modern Japanese family law. In Law in Japan. Arthur Taylor Von Mehren, ed. Cambridge, Mass.: Harvard University Press.

Wigmore, John Henry. 1969ff. Law and justice in Tokugawa Japan: Part 5, Property -- civil and customary law; Pt. 7, Persons -- civil and customary law. Tokyo: University of Tokyo Press.

Wimberly, Howard. 1973. On living with your past: Style structure among contemporary Japanese merchant families. Economic Development and Cultural Change 21:423-428.

Yamada, Masao. 1984. Kibitamura ni ikita hitobito (The people who lived in Kibita village). Kobe: Kobe Shinbun Shuppan Senta.

Yamamura, Kozo. 1985. Samurai income and demographic change: The geneologies of Tokugawa Bannermen. In Family and population in east Asian history. Susan Hanley and Arthur Wolf, eds. Stanford: Stanford University Press.

Yamamura, Kozo and Susan B. Hanley. 1972. Quantitative data for Japanese economic history. In The Dimensions of the past. Val L. Lorwin and Jacob M. Price, eds. New Haven: Yale University Press.

Yamamura, Kozo and Susan B. Hanley. 1975. Ichihime, ni Tarō: Educational aspirations and the decline in fertility in post-war Japan. Journal of Japanese Studies 2:83-125.

Yamamura, Masae. 1975. Chokkeisei kazoku ni okeru kaku bunri (An analysis of separation of nuclear units within a stem family in a rural community). Shakaigaku Hyōron (Japanese Sociological Review) 102:18-35.

Yamamura, Yoshiaki. 1983. Nihon no oya, Nihon no katei (Japanese parents, Japanese families). Tokyo: Kaneko Shobō.

Yamamuro, Shūhei. 1973. Kazoku to wa nani ka (What is the family). In Kazoku Hendō no Shakaigaku (Sociology of family change). Kazuo Aoi and Masuda Kōkichi, eds. Tokyo: Baifūkan.

Yamamuro, Shūhei. 1978. Review of Kakukazoku saikō (Rethinking the nuclear family), by Tsubouchi Yoshihiro and Maeda Naribumi. Kazoku Kenkyū Nenpō (Annals of Family Studies) 4:66-68.

Yamamuro, Shūhei. 1981. Tōda Teizō no kazoku gakusetsu (Tōda Teizō's theory of the family). Kazoku Shi Kenkyū (Studies in Family History) 4:126-149.

Yamamuro, Shūhei and Himeoka Tsutomu, eds. 1970. Gendai kazoku no shakaigaku (The sociology of the modern family). Tokyo: Baifūkan.

Yamanaka, Miyuki. 1976. Dokkyo rōjin to kinjō no kankei (The elderly who live alone and their neighborhood relations). Kazoku Kenkyū Nenpō (Annals of Family Studies) 2:59-71.

Yamanaka, Miyuki. 1981. Shinzoku kankei (Kin relations). In Nihonjin no kazoku kankei (Japanese family relations). Kamiko Takeji and Masuda Kōkichi, eds. Tokyo: Yūhikaku.

Yamane, Tsuneo and Nonoyama Hisaya. 1967. Nippon ni okeru kakukazoku no koritsu to shinzoku sōshiki (Isolation of the nuclear family and kinship organization in Japan). Shakaigaku Hyōron (Japanese Sociological Review) 69:64-84.

Yamashita, Kesao. 1979. Rōnen no kazoku fuyō ni oyobasu shakai hendō no eikyō (The impact of social change on family support of the elderly). Rōnen Shakai Kagaku (Japanese Journal of Gerontology) 1:23-30.

Yamate, Shigeru. 1978. Review of Kazoku no shakaigaku (Family sociology), by Iida Tetsuya. Kazoku Kenkyū Nenpō (Annals of Family Studies) 4:69-71.

Yanase, Toshiyuki. 1972. The koseki as a source for the scholar of Japan. In Studies in Asian geneology. Spencer J. Palmer, ed. Provo, Utah: Brigham Young University Press.

Yōda, Seiichi and Toshitani Nobuyoshi. 1977. Shutōken no kaihatsu to nōka no kazoku, zaisan kankei no henka (Changes in the relations of farm family and property in developing areas near Tokyo). In Kazoku: Seisaku to hō 3, Sengo Nihon kazoku no dōkō. Fukishima Masao, ed. Tokyo: University of Tokyo Press.

Yokoe, Katsumi. 1970. Historical trends in home discipline. In Families in east and west. Reuben Hill and René Konig, eds. The Hague: Mouton.

Yokoyama, Minoru. 1979. Review of Gendai kazoku no raifu saikuru, Morioka Kiyomi, ed. Kazoku Kenkyū Nenpō (Annals of Family Studies) 5:73-75.

Yokoyama, Sadao. 1949. Kinsei tōshi shūraku no dōtaisei to shūdansei (Movement and groupings in the urban community of the early modern period). In Gendai shakaigaku no shōmondai (Problems of modern sociology). Tokyo: Kōbundō.

Yuzawa, Yasuhiko. 1972. Kazoku sutoresu to seikatsu kōzō (Family stress and life structure). In Shakaigaku kōza 3: Kazoku shakaigaku. Morioka Kiyomi, ed. Tokyo: University of Tokyo Press.

Yuzawa, Yasuhiko. 1975. Ochanomizu de no gojū-nen (50 Years at Ochanomizu). Special issue on Kōnenrei o ikiru (The life of old people). No. 7. Chiiki Shakai Kenkyūshō.

Yuzawa, Yasuhiko. 1977a. Rōjin mondai to rōshin fuyō no dōkō (The problem of the elderly and trends in the support of elderly parents). In Kazoku: Seisaku to hō 3, Sengo Nihon kazoku no dōkō. Fukishima Masao, ed. Tokyo: University of Tokyo Press.

Yuzawa, Yasuhiko. 1977b. Sengo kazoku hendō no tōkeiteki kansatsu (Statistical consideration of post-war family change). In Kazoku: Seisaku to hō 3, Sengo Nihon kazoku no dōkō. Fukishima Masao, ed. Tokyo: University of Tokyo Press.

Yuzawa, Yasuhiko. 1978. Sanson josei no seikatsu hendō (The life change of women in a mountain village). Special issue on Komyuniti (Community). No. 52. Chiiki Shakai Kenkyūsho.

Yuzawa, Yasuhiko. 1981. Kengyō nōka no otoshiyoritachi (The old people living in a farm village). Special issue on Kōnenrei o ikiru (The life of old people). No. 14. Chiiki Shakai Kenkyūshō.

INDEX OF JAPANESE TERMS

Japanese Term	Rough English Equivalent	Page on which introduced
bunke	branch family	9
chokkei kazoku	lineal family, stem	7
dōzoku	hierarchical group of households	9
honke	main family	9
ie	corporate lineal family	7
inkyō	retirement	58
kazoku	family	7
koseki	family register	20
miai	arranged marriage	42
renai	"love marriage"	42
shinrui (shinseki, shinzoku)	kindred, relatives	10
shitsuke	child-rearing, discipline	54
shūmonchō	Tokugawa period population register	19
shusei chokkei kazoku	modified lineal family	68
yōshi	adopted heir	8

CORNELL UNIVERSITY EAST ASIA SERIES

No. 2 China's Green Revolution by Benedict Stavis

No. 4 Provincial Leadership in China: The Cultural Revolution and Its Aftermath by Fredrick Teiwes

No. 8 Vocabulary and Notes to Ba Jin's *Jia*: An Aid for Reading the Novel by Cornelius C. Kubler

No. 14 Black Crane 1: An Anthology of Korean Literature edited by David R. McCann

No. 15 Song, Dance, Storytelling: Aspects of the Performing Arts in Japan by Frank Hoff

No. 16 Nō as Performance: An Analysis of the Kuse Scene of *Yamamba* by Monica Bethe and Karen Brazell (videotapes available)

No. 17 Pining Wind: A Cycle of Nō Plays translated by Royall Tyler

No. 18 Granny Mountains: A Second Cycle of Nō Plays translated by Royall Tyler

No. 21 Three Works by Nakano Shigeharu translated by Brett de Bary

No. 22 The Tale of Nezame: Part Three of Yowa no Nezame Monogatari translated by Carol Hochstedler

No. 23 Nanking Letters, 1949 by Knight Biggerstaff

No. 25 Four Japanese Travel Diaries of the Middle Ages translated by Herbert Plutschow and Hideichi Fukuda

No. 27 The Jurchens in the Yüan and Ming by Morris Rossabi

No. 28 The Griffis Collection of Japanese Books: An Annotated Bibliography edited by Diane E. Perushek

No. 29   Dance in the Nō Theater   by Monica Bethe and Karen Brazell
          Volume 1: Dance Analysis
          Volume 2: Plays and Scores
          Volume 3: Dance Patterns
          (videotapes available)

No. 30   Irrigation Management in Japan: A Critical Review of Japanese Social
          Science Research   by William W. Kelly

No. 31   Water Control in Tokugawa Japan: Irrigation Organization in a Japanese
          River Basin, 1600-1870   by William W. Kelly

No. 32   Tone, Segment, and Syllable in Chinese: A Polydimensional Approach to
          Surface Phonetic Structure   by A. Ronald Walton

No. 35   From Politics to Lifestyles: Japan in Print, I   edited by Frank Baldwin

No. 36   The Diary of a Japanese Innkeeper's Daughter   translated by Miwa Kai
          edited and annotated by Robert J. Smith and Kazuko Smith

No. 37   International Perspectives on Yanagita Kunio and Japanese Folklore Studies
          edited by J. Victor Koschmann, Ōiwa Keibō and Yamashita Shinji

No. 38   Murō Saisei: Three Works   translated by James O'Brien

No. 40   Land of Volcanic Ash: A Play in Two Parts by Kubo Sakae   translated
          by David G. Goodman

No. 41   The Dreams of Our Generation and Selections from Beijing's People
          by Zhang Xinxin   edited and translated by Edward Gunn, Donna Jung
          and Patricia Farr

No. 42   From Politics to Lifestyles: Japan in Print, II   edited by Frank Baldwin

No. 43   Post-War Japanese Resource Policies and Strategies: The Case of
          Southeast Asia   by Shoko Tanaka

No. 44   Family Change and the Life Course in Japan   by Susan Orpett Long

No. 45   Regulatory Politics in Japan: The Case of Foreign Banking
          by Louis W. Pauly

No. 46   Planning and Finance in China's Economic Reforms
          by Thomas P. Lyons and WANG Yan

No. 48   Bungo Manual: Selected Reference Materials for Students of Classical
          Japanese   by Helen Craig McCullough

No. 49   Ankoku Butō: The Premodern and Postmodern Influences on the Dance of Utter Darkness   by Susan Blakeley Klein

No. 50   Twelve Plays of the Noh and Kyōgen Theaters   edited by Karen Brazell

No. 51   Five Plays by Kishida Kunio   edited by David Goodman

No. 52   Ode to Stone   by Shirō Hara   translated by James Morita

For information on ordering the preceding publications and videotapes, please write to:

EAST ASIA SERIES
East Asia Program
Cornell University
140 Uris Hall
Ithaca, NY 14853-7601

3-91 .4M U

2 04